KALYUG CHRONICLES BOOK-I

SERVANT OF THE ETERNAL

AUTHOR

NIHARIKA SAHU

Acknowledgment

Writing a book is easy but writing a story is not an easy job. It took me more than a year to research and then plot a story based on the myths. One complete year I isolated myself from the outer world, which was honestly not an easy job but the outcome is in front of you. I wrote this story alone but I was not alone. Outstanding people with their magnificent imagination helped me to complete this book, directly or indirectly. I want to thank those souls who were there in my journey.

My parents, who supported me through every thick and thin. Coming from a conservative society, they always encouraged me to spread my wings. Especially, my father who never saw me as daughter, who needs to be protected but as an independent girl who knows what she is doing with her life. Leaving my full time job in a big company and writing this book was not an easy decision but their support and their faith in me, made it possible.

My sisters Neha and Nidhi, Who encouraged me to think out of the box and pushed me to complete this book.

Nidhi Sahu and Divya Tondon, my editors , for their excellent editing work and making my pedestrian English worth reading.

Vikram Bajpai, for the beautiful cover design.

Amrit Ravidya Raj, for his motivating words that kept me believing in myself.

Dharmendra Singh, for being my first reader and critic.

My dog, Frodo for never leaving me alone for a minute and listening the story again and again, without any complains.

Speacial thanks to Kaavyarth for writing those heart touching poems in the letter.

Lastly, to the one God I worshipped my entire life. Who brought me back from the state of depression and my firm believe in his existence also made me believe in a world beyond this world.

Special Thanks

I thank you from the bottom of my heart to the legendary pop and country singer and song writer **Bobby Goldsboro** for giving me permission to use the lyrics of his chartbuster song ***"Broomstick cowboy"***.
Because without this song my book would have never been complete. Also, thank you for this lovely message. You will always be my favourite Artist. I will never forget the day when I received this email from you.

 Dear Niharika,

Thanks so much for your touching email. We showed it to Bobby. He said to tell you this:

"Dear Niharika,

I am honored that you would want to use my lyrics to ***"Broomstick Cowboy"*** in you novel. You have my permission and my blessing. I wish you great success.

Sincerely,
Bobby Goldsboro"

Bobby Goldsboro Productions

Kalyug chronicles:

In this materialistic world, Belief is a myth. A myth like our Gods. With the beginning of an era the Gods we believed once existed in this earth have abandoned us and turned their backs on us.

What if we are wrong? What if they are just sitting somewhere waiting for us to give up on ourselves? Or they are waiting for us to finally accept our sins? What if they are so disappointed in their own creations that they want us to be destroyed by the hand of an Evil? An evil so strong, stronger than any other demon that ever existed in the earth.

Kalyug chronicles is the story which starts with a forbidden love story which holds the key to the mysterious world and ends with an epic war that world has ever seen.

'Servant of the Eternal' is the story of the redemption of a long lost warrior who is surviving his cursed life under the shadow. It is the first book of the series followed by three more books in the coming years with many known characters of our mythologies.

My Love,

Every story has a hero, who comes to rescue his love. But our story was different, in our story we rescued each other from our past and together we built a future for ourselves.

Every year we ended up little broken and every year we mended a little more. Your love is like vintage wine, intoxicating me more as old as it gets. It was in your arms when my soul took its first breath and my peace was in the chaos of your love.

But we were living in dreams, dreams where our hearts found solace. Baby, I love you with all your flaws because they make you a perfect lover!

Every time, my heart skips a beat when your breath falls on my skin. You embraced me like a flower accepting an eternal fall of dew drop.

Today, I can see beyond our love. I see both of us, together.

I am resting in your arms, you are holding my palms. I guess this is our forever.

We never vowed to take our last breath together but we will always be each other's soul mates, forever.

Tomorrow, I might be gone but I will always love you. Just like a dead flower still holds its sweet smell between the weathered pages of a book.

The innocent soul in front of you will melt your pain of the lost love, soon.

Love never lasts....it stays, forever.

Love,
Abeedah.

PROLOGUE

Bhāgavata Purāṇa 3.32.8-10 says-

"Ashwathaama Balirvyaaso Hanumanshcha Vibheeshanaha

Krupaha Parshuramascha Saptaitey Chiranjivinaha

Saptaitaan Samsmareynnityam Markandeymathaashtamam

Jivedvarshshatam Sopi Sarvavyadhivivarjit"

A man was praying at the altar, grieving his father. He was holding the urn in his hands clutched to his chest, which contained his beloved father's ashes close to his chest. He was in denial at first, couldn't believe that his father was dead, even though he saw him falling unconscious in front of his own eyes, his head falling on the ground, eyes closed.

Then came the rage, the rage that killed thousands of men in his wake. Now he was in grief, a soul-crushing sadness, challenging his sanity. He lost the last of his conscience when he saw his friend who was more of a brother, murdered at the hands of Bhima on the last day of the Mahabharata.

His righteous soul was shadowed by the burning need for vengeance, to avenge his father and his beloved friend deaths and his lividness has taken over his consciousness.

The last three survivors of Kaurava clan decided to kill those who played dirty to win the war, who broke all the rules to win. The night has been dark just like the future they see for themselves. But the Gods were protecting their enemies. Bhairav was standing at the door providing a protective shield to Pandavas.

The furious warrior prayed to Lord Shiva, his patron God and Goddess Parvati with such dedication that they couldn't resist themselves to hear his prayer and granted him with the boon of their blessing. He offered himself to

Mahakaal's possession and Kali by his side, with the Chandrahas sword in his hand, which seeks nothing but blood.

He was undefeatable. The undefeatable grieving warrior with his friend and uncle slaughtered the last of Pandavas in the palace.

But Krishna was a step ahead of him. He escaped the five Pandava brothers with their wife Panchali before the massacre started. Missing the primary targets made the warrior livid and ashamed of killing Droupatis sons. By the sunrise, the pandavas found the warrior and attempted to attack him with the most potent Astra he had in his knowledge, the Brahmastra.

Arjuna to counter his attack, intended to use the same Astra. Vyasa and Krishna, worried about the destruction of whole mankind, suggested both the archers to take back their Astra. Arjuna accepted the suggestion and enchanted to revoke his Brahmastra. But on the other hand, the lack of knowledge to revoke the arrow made the warrior to direct it to the most vulnerable target, an unborn child in the womb of Uttara, the last bit of Abhimanyu. Abhimanyu, Arjuna's son and the last heir of Pandav bloodline, brutally killed by his own uncles inside the Chakravyuh. His death was the most brutal killing in the history of Mahabharata. The brutality followed its trail to his son life too, resulted in the death of an innocent life inside his mother's womb.

Such inhuman behaviour angered Krishna. Lord Krishna well known for his rock solid decisions and a well-known punisher, punished the last sinner of the Kaurava clan.

Lord Krishna's voice boomed in the air, "Curse you, you shrewd man, who did the unthinkable horror of killing an unborn child! I curse you that you will carry the burden of people's sins on your shoulders and will roam alone like a ghost without getting any love and curtsy until the end of Kalyug.

You will have neither hospitality nor any accommodation. You will be in total isolation from humankind and society. Your body will suffer from the host of incurable disease, forming sores and ulcers that will never heal. You may lead the most wretched life anyone can ever lead. May you never receive love or affection ever in your life into the end of time."

His words echoed in the air, and his curse left the immortal warrior alone in the dark pit of suffering for eternity. The warrior lost everything with this curse and death was all he wanted, and now, even that was not his to embrace. Every boon crosses their path with a curse, and every curse crosses their path with a blessing, though he was not sure of it anymore.

Lord Krishna, the clairvoyant that he was, knew that this curse would take to make him fulfil his destiny, for his part will be the beginning of the most significant prophecy to save humankind. But the warrior, unaware of his fate, fell on his knees, only a single tear escaping his eyes.

Lord Krishna showed his mercy to the heirless thrown of Hastinapur, because he knew how important it was to have an heir who will rule Hastinapur till the dusk of Dwaparyug. He saw the agonising pain of a mother who lost his son before breathing his first air in the world. Krishna resurrected the left soul and heartbeat of the deadbeat again. He named him Parikshit. Lord Krishna knew King Parikshit would never allow Kali of Kalyug to enter the border of his kingdom till his last breath.

For the immortal archer, even the change of Yuga couldn't bring an end to his suffering. The suffering which he had to bear alone. A boon of immortality, which he was born with was now a never-ending suffering which he cannot escape. He is currently nothing but the Servant of Eternal.

Glossary

Chapter One

we are here, together...

The season of winter is a fresh dew drop in nature's lap. This was the time of the year adores the serene beauty of our life. A day of sunshine and the sky faded in blue seems like an outbreak of view from autumn. This season reminds of the happiness of iftari, the food consumed by Muslims post-sunset during the festival of Ramadan, after starving a long day.

Though every season has its specialty, winter is that cold breeze which mesmerises our soul. Winter times in Mumbai were entirely different from other states. Not too harsh, which develops the urge for hugging woolen clothes and clattering of teeth. It had a soft windy climate which nobody could get over it.

This season of winter reminds Abeedah of the changes in her life. She could feel the breeze touching her skin and leaving her with a delicate awareness of it. Such is the feeling she waited for and never had for a long time. A view from her smudged window showed the signs of a new life. Those bare branches were brewing tiny buds of oxygen. Life has started evolving again on those branches. Few petals are developing while some flowers are playing with the cool breeze just like a new-born plays with his toys.

Abeedah stretched out her fingers from the window to feel the softness of those silky pink petals. Undoubtedly, winter is quite clement with those little lives. It was way softer than her expectation and too delicate to enjoy its softness for a longer time. Sadly, nature has its own cycle, and these little flowers will fall to signify that one cannot bend the destiny of change. Abeedah was not ready to face such change. She happily lost in the sudden turn of nature.

During this season, Abeedah craved for the touch of those wet grass under the warm sun. This mixture of experiencing warmth and coldness together used to rejuvenate her. She imagined herself of climbing a ladder to get a more elegant sense of this winter-aroma. The street light reminds her of tiredness to look at the artificial light. The twilight use to welcome her whenever she used to leave for home from the hospital.

It was Abeedah's earnest desire to witness a peaceful sunset. She craved for a view of a faded orange sky; birds returning to their nest just like Abeedah would be going back to her nest. She wanted to share this familiar feeling with the sunset, but alas, her responsibilities were too heavy to let her do those.

It was a beautiful morning on Sunday, and she wanted to spend her quality time in tranquility and away from the noise of the city. Living in Mumbai is quite challenging, but with such dreams and desires of calmness, it escalates the level of challenges. Abeedah could feel the difference in her hopes and the other citizens of Mumbai. They were unknown faces which used to cross her path daily, but their aspirations were known to her. Strange, but not too unusual.

It is a city of colours, and everyone wants to achieve their goals, earning a name from it. While she was lost in such kind of feeling, on the contrary, her fiancé, Shad, and her friends had their desires. They all were planning a trip to visit Chhattisgarh, a state located in the heart of India. It was Abeedah who proposed the idea to visit this land because she wants to visit this little piece of paradise, Chitrakoot waterfall situated in that state.

One of her colleagues showed his holiday snaps of this place and called it the "Niagara falls of India." It was since then she was mesmerised by its serene beauty and felt a sudden knock in her heart as if she can't afford not to visit this place. Since that moment, she was feeling a strange kind of attraction towards such place. Perhaps she founded a gateway to fulfilling her desires through this Chitrakoot waterfall.

They were planning the trip for the summer, and after such a long wait, their wait was finally over. It was a rare destination in between the chaos of this world.

Shad was very excited for the trip as it was going to be the first official trip as a couple after they got hitched. After pursuing his post-graduation from Buffalo University in computer science, then working for two years with corporate office, it was indeed a much-needed vacation to experience the scenery with the closest person in his life.

Shad and Abeedah met at a camp of healthcare where he was a volunteer for an NGO and Abeedah was the doctor-in-charge. Their destiny crossed their paths while dealing with a severe case.

Shad was a handsome man. His fair complexion complimented his mischievous brown eyes surrounded by thick eyelashes. Those eyes were worth the stare. His nerdy black glasses highlighted his eyes even more. His shiny and bouncy brown hair made you itch to run fingers through them. There was informality in his personality, a certain casualness which was entirely contrasting his outfit which was always on the mark, which he paid a lot of attention to. He had a tall face which used to reflect his high level of confidence.

It was the collectivity of his charming demeanor, his character and looks which makes Shad a very desirable man. Abeedah noticed the intensity in his eyes which others failed to. She saw a sense of gentleness and decency from it which stands above the discussions of any shade. Yes, it had on Shad's face that this man is not accustomed to losing anything in which he is involved. Abeedah noticed all these qualities of Shad when they were treating a case. Gradually, they became friends, and their friendship took the next level of dating with the pace of time.

Shad was all in all what Abeedah used to seek in her life partner. Apart from being smart and handsome, he was equally sensitive and caring being a human. Abeedah got attracted towards the qualities of him being a kind-hearted person. We all feel the need of a safe harbor, a divine love in our life where we can sail our life's boat without any sense of fear. Without love, everything around feels like a burden on the soul. Without love, people only survive but fail to live their life. Gradually it turns into a feeling of torture which Abeedah had endured all her life till now.

They planned to leave by eleven in the morning. Shad's excitement for the trip was reflected, apparently, while he was packing his bags and deciding his outfits. He planned to have a separate outfit for each day. It was supposed to be a seven days trip. Shad was very particular when it comes to his attire. He was not one jean on every occasion kind of a guy while Abeedah was quite practical when it comes to her packing. She was very particular on choosing the essential items needed for the trip.

As Abeedah's profession demanded, she was well versed in her skills of deciding what is the most critical and which is the least is. This time, she had a single bag with the right quality and quantity of stuff in it. It was irrespective of whether it is a one day or a seven days trip. She never forgets to apply her scientific knowledge in her practical aspects of life.

With their entire luggage, they waited for their best friends, Ragini and her husband, Siddhant to join them. Siddhant's bottomless black eyes were precise enough to make a person feel lost. Sometimes he used to control his blinking of eyes and used to get stuck at a point. This situation always seemed as if Siddhant was hypnotized. Ragini used to make fun of him that he loves to be in his own la-la land.

Two years back Abeedah joined the hospital along with Ragini and Siddhant, although Ragini and Abeedah were college buddies. And what always happen to the group of three, happened with them also. Ragini and Siddhant started spending more time together and within few months of their friendship, Ragini informed Abeedah about her relationship with Siddhant.

The relationship was understandable but what Abeedah was not able to swallow was Ragini's sudden decision of marrying Siddhant, which finally made sense when Ragini revealed the secret after Abeedah had confronted her about the pregnancy test. Nevertheless, Siddhant had an engaging personality, and he cared for Ragini. They seemed to be a happily married couple.

Ragini came from an orthodox Christian family carrying a true Indian heart. She was more inclined towards Indian culture and its customs. Her wardrobe was full of Indian attires, and she used to carry it very gracefully.

It was supposed to be a long journey. So, they decided to start the trip early to reach before the morning of the upcoming day. Shad was loading the luggage in the car boot while Abeedah was waiting for Ragini and Siddhant. It was 11:30 a.m. and the sun was gradually heading towards their head. There was no sign of any fresh breeze or a cloud which could have blocked the attack of sun's rays on them. She curled her fingers around the thin fabric of her top, waving it in and out to create a little air flow. But it was not enough to save her from the heat. Her head was figuratively reaching to the boiling point because of the black color hijab she was wearing, she mentioned Shad

Abeedah was having a tough time to even think about why her friends had not shown up yet. The sun's heat was solely enough to keep her busy facing it. Eyes set to the horizon, arms resting on the cold metal rail, that's when after two hours of wait they heard, teasing Shad for his over packing. Finally, they have arrived.

"Dude, we are going for four days. Four! Not for an entire month! Abeedah is carrying just one, and you have two suitcases?" said Siddhant with a mouthful laugh.

"I just like to be prepared. That's it," said Shad shyly. Their entire luggage was loaded and they started their journey with an excitement level at its peak. It was fun getting along with friends and going on a road trip. Abeedah was having the time of her life. She was having her people who loved her. At that moment, she said to herself "This is it, all I ever wanted!" She never wanted this adventure to end.

Siddhant aligned his face to the window pane to catch a glimpse of the prism of sunlight scattering on the window's surface. It was a long journey, and Abeedah was already missing her daily routine. She was going to her appointment diary to check her daily logs, what she had canceled or didn't bother to cancel. It was by midnight of the same day when they touched the border of Chhattisgarh.

Winter in this state was entirely different from that of Mumbai. It felt like nature had taken a sudden turn in the air of Chhattisgarh. All Abeedah felt, was sheer cold. As a result, she folded her legs up and covered them with her arms to fight the chill. This action of her made her appear as a butterfly entering into a cocoon. The warmth of her body and the coldness on her face, made her feel good. The heat in her body and the chill was now quite balanced. They decided to temporary halt their journey till the sunrise and rest their heads in a hotel near the highway.

The next morning they saw the white sky in contrast to the blue sky. A sense of laziness was present in the cool breeze. It was flowing across wildly without any purpose and beyond any destination. Shad looked out of the door, to witness the vibrant feeling of the morning. He pulled out his thin cardigan around himself and called everyone to begin a fresh start.

After the traditional breakfast, they started their journey again.
"The food was good but I think people in here don't like spicy food." Shad made a comment and started the car.

It didn't take long that the dry color of white faded, and the sky welcomed the sun for his daily ritual. Abeedah always wondered that why the highway looks wet and shiny off in the distance but dry enough as one gets closer to the same position. Sadly the philosophy of mirage was too near to leave a mark on her life. Shad was driving, and Abeedah sat beside him. Siddhant and Ragini were getting comfortable in the back seat.

"Such a lovely couple they are.." Abeedah whispered to Shad.

"Don't worry sweetheart; we are not that bad either." Shad chuckled.
In the midst of their whispering, Ragini started teasing Shad.

"Shad, you are one lucky man! All these years and I have never seen Abeedah letting anyone this close to her skin" she said teasing Shad.
They all were in the mood for fun. Abeedah turned back and tried to push Ragini by her shoulder. "Stop it! Ragini" said Abeedah.

"Ok fine. Answer me this, Abeedah. How much do you love Shad?" Ragini asked.
"Ragini, love can never be quantified and weighed. Try asking a practical question next time!" Abeedah replied.

"Then what makes you stick together with Shad?" She asked
"It is the concept of compatibility behind ours being together. And because of this compatibility, we fell in love?" Abeedah answered giving a snob and questioning expression to Shad.

On hearing this, Shad raised his eyebrow and implored Abeedah. "That means you were not in love with me initially?"
Ragini and Siddhant giggled at the back seat in the most playful way.

Abeedah replied with a soft and a confident voice "I think love, at first sight, is a myth, neither love is blind. We look for compatibility and choose our partner?" She replied.
Shad nodded and asked "So if I did not have a good job, not living in Mumbai and was an ugly man, you wouldn't have fallen in love with me because I was not

compatible with you. Is it so?"

She retaliated. "No! My love was not because of your job or you being handsome or any other thing which you have mentioned. It was because you were kind, polite and a very caring person. I got attracted to these qualities of yours." Shad looked at her frowning face and said, "Honey, I am sorry. I never meant to disrespect you or your thoughts. I was just pulling your leg. It doesn't matter to me which path we are on to reach the destination… what matters is we are here, together."

She blushed. She could not hide her smile under anger.
Ragini and Siddhant, "Come on guys, no more serious discussions. You both carry on with your romance and fights once we are back to Mumbai." They all laughed.

Chapter Two

But I firmly believe God exist

They reached their destination by the afternoon. As they stepped outside the car, a gush of heat surrounded their body like a hot-blooded serpent twist itself around the bark. Even the ground on which they were stepping was giving a burning sensation to their feet which they felt through their footwear.

"It is strange how the night is so cold, and daytime is hot like summer days. Strange place!" Shad noted.

The sun was up above their head soaking all their energies, but the sight was heavenly enough to feel the heat beneath their feet. They decided to clean their dirt and sweat in a restroom. They had some fruits to fill their stomach and started the tour. The place was calm like a meditation centre which reminded them of Malgudi days.

At a distance the folk song was being played in the loudspeaker, the language was not understandable, but they guessed it was a song praising some Mother Karma because these two words were only words they understood.

On their way, they saw a farmer on the roadside. A dark-skinned, skinny person, ribs easily visible through his body. He was wearing a dhoti and a turban to cover his head from the heat. Sadly, he could not save his bare body which had undergone tanning. They approached him and luckily he could understand their language. His name was Chagan. Shad asked him about the Chitrakoot fall. Apart from helping them with directions, Chagan entertained them with lots of information about the place in his local language. Which was not that difficult to understand after putting some efforts.

"How far is the city from here?" Siddhant asked,

"Not too far." Chagan replied.

"Is the whole state like this?" Ragini asked.

"No, there are many big cities entirely different from this place. We don't get many tourists here."

"Why?" Ragini asked curiously. But, Chagan distracted them with his many stories.

Apparently, he seem too excited to see the tourists which made him think that it was his duty to act as a guide and provide as much information as he could.

Meanwhile, Ragini asked him, "What is this song about; the music is unusual but very catchy? The tune stuck in my head. Who is this Karma? Is this 'KARMA' Karma?" She made air quotes with her fingers.

Ragini had this habit of attaching her memories to some song or smell. So that, whenever she listens to that song, she relives the feeling of the moment. Chagan narrated the lyrics and told her the story of Lady Karma who was a devotee of Krishna.

"I heard the story as a child by my Grandmother. The story of little girl named Karmabai. The lore says Karmabai's father was a devotee of Lord Krishna. Once upon a time, he had some work outstation, so he instructed the little girl to offer the food to the lord and then only she should eat.

Karma was a young girl who was obedient to his father. Her fragile mind took this instruction literally. Next morning when she woke up, she followed the instructions given by her father with all her heart. She made the khichri as an offering to the idol of Lord Krishna. But when she saw that the statue was not eating, sincere towards her father's request innocent Karmabai did not eat anything at all and waited for the lord to come and eat.

Lord Krishna, impressed by her determination and innocence, showed mercy on her. He appeared before her and ate the khichri with her hand. She followed the same routine every day, till her father returned home.

After her father returned she told him everything that happened, her father was shocked in disbelief and refused to believe in her story. Thus karma pleaded lord to appear once again to prove her truth. And very merciful Lord Krishna did seem once again to keep his devotee's respect."

After narrating the story, he said, "There is a community here who worship her like a Goddess. Well it's just a story, we pray Gods and Goddess every day for rain, for food but he doesn't seem to be bothered much." Chagan had this sadness in his eyes which defined his condition but the most impressive thing about him was he never left his smile behind. Shad tried to give him some cash for as a curtsy but the poor farmer refused it saying, "We treat guests as Gods. So, we can't take any money for the hospitality." And he left for his work.

As they got back in the car, Ragini said, "I liked the story. But I think Chagan is right. I don't believe that such things actually happened in reality." While they left for the place from which they were few kilometres away.

Abeedah continued, "Maybe. But I firmly believe God exist"

After half an hour of driving on an uneven, muddy road, they reached the location. The very first glimpse of the waterfall was magnificent. It was so high to locate its beginning point. It was more like directly falling from the sky. The water tumbled down the hillside which was so bright to eyes, in a series of mini-waterfalls. Its flow tinkled in the form of a child's laughter. From a distance, it appeared like a silent white stream falling over the rocky projections.

The closer they came, the louder was the noise of the fall. They stood few meters away from it and could barely hear each other's voice because of the thunderous roar of the water. The rocks were slippery due to the layer of green algae on it.

But there was an iron rope for the support to cross the stream. They stood at a permissible distance and still could feel the vapors and shrinking water droplets at them. It was a moment of magic, no less than a heaven for them.

A new place to visit and an extraordinary land, but its calmness was quite familiar to Abeedah. Its calm greenery was rejuvenating her senses. They descended to the shallow end of the fall, and nobody could resist jumping into it. Shad jumped, Ragini and Siddhant followed him. They insisted Abeedah to join but she couldn't because of her terrible fear of deep waters. She halfheartedly sat on a nearby rock, enjoying the scenery from a distance. She found her joy looking at Shad and her friends' faces filled with giggles.

She looked around the area and saw that, upon the forest floor lies trees of yesteryear, fallen in storms. She walked into it. It was the orchestra of her mind, playing one enchanting symphony after another. The leaves danced to an unheard beat, whispering their songs to the afternoon wind.

The place around her was enriched in flora. Her eyes fell on a particular flower. She had a hard time remembering its name but it was a rare flower with medicinal properties. The localities were probably unaware of it and how valuable it was. It was a beautiful flower with deep red petals. There were other exquisite flowers nearby, and Abeedah started following them.

"Abeedah, where are you going?" Shad shouted.

"Just watching some flowers, I'll be right back!" she shouted back.

He yelled an okay, and she went off following the trail of those flowers. The forest was dense enough to hide the brightness of the sky. Only a few fragments of blue glimpsed like scattered pieces of an impossible jigsaw puzzle. She found it strange that the place wasn't populated. It indeed wasn't a favorite tourist spot as Chagan mentioned.

The site gave her a moment of silence. Enough of Peace to wonder who Abeedah Hassan was! Long chestnut brown hair always covered by Hijab, It is a cloth which is used by Muslim women to cover their head in public. And chocolate brown eyes and a lean figure, she wasn't gorgeous physically, unlike Shad. Her features were delicate with a small button nose, almond eyes and a heart-shaped face with dusky complexion. A little mole teased her upper lips. Abeedah always felt a little undermined whenever she used to be in public with Shad. Shad but loved her simple looks and that helped her in overcoming this complex. When it comes to her personality, her beauty takes a backseat before it. She was a kind woman with an adventurous heart. Her dry sense of humor used to make Shad laugh out so hard that he used to fell from his seat.

She heard an unusual chirping; she looked around and saw a small colorful, beautiful bird sitting on a branch. After sitting for a couple of seconds, it winged towards a direction. Abeedah, mesmerized by that bird's beauty, followed her. After some time, she found herself in the middle of a small isolated piece of land surrounded by some ancient caves. She was lost.

The trees were thick and old. Its roots were so twisted that it was impossible to untangle it. It would have once filled with bird-songs and animals. But now, it ages had passed its former glory. What it's covering was so dense that one could only see the occasional streak of sunlight that barely touched the forest floor. Even its thick vines were gradually swallowing the last fragments of the temple that stood in the centre.

She moved forward to look for a way back to the waterfall when the forest echoed with the sound of a gunshot. Until now she was unaware of how the shots sounded in reality. She had only heard them in the counterstrike games, which Shad used to play quite often. She had even used a gun but just in such games. This sound was not similar to the ones which they used to hear in the game. It was way louder than her imagination. She followed the sound, ran as fast as she could to the spot where she left Shad, Ragini and Siddhant . She stood behind a tree and watched the scene unfold in front of her. Fear gripped her heart when her eyes got stuck at a site where a group of men and women with guns, standing at a distance. One of the ladies in the khaki pant had a gun over Shad. They looked like bandits, who harass people for money and valuables. The more she observed them, more brutal they seemed to be. Their intention was not just the money, they believed in torturing people.

Ragini was crying for help, and Shad was trying to talk to them, calmly. Abeedah looked around for Siddhant, but he was nowhere in the vicinity. Shad caught a glimpse of Abeedah peeping from behind the trunk and gestured her to hide.

She wanted to help them, but they were loaded with weapons. Finally, she stood up and courageously threw a big piece of rock at one of the bandits. But this was an action that was going to cost her dearly. No sooner the rock hit the lady, she lost her control and pulled the trigger, shooting Shad. The bullet pierced his skin expanding from the supersonic impact to the size of a coin. For few seconds, the sound of the gunshot echoed in her ears, and the whole world stood still, everything in her life was collapsing into that music. She saw the life draining out of Shad in his eyes as his lifeless body fell to the ground with a thud. Before she could pull herself together, they killed Ragini with the second shot.

When she saw her best friend blown out in the furrow, she screamed her name. Everyone turned towards her and started firing bullet after bullet. She started running into blind terror and was panicking. She ran towards the direction of those caves. Dodging those bullets, she hid behind a pile of rock. She could feel her destiny approaching and was just waiting for it to get over. She thought no sooner; they would find and shoot her.

It was after sunset, and her survival became more difficult due to the darkness. With every footstep approaching her made a pitching echo because of the mud and water. Some strange sound was also echoing around her. By the fall of every foot and crunching of dry leaves, her heart pounded to blast. She attempted to run and but fell unconscious after hitting her head with a piece of rock. She could sense her death nearby.

Subconsciously, she accepted it even before fighting. She could see Shad's face in front of her eyes and the very next scene of his body lying in the pool of his own blood, eyes dead. There was no reason left for her to live in this world. She could count her heartbeat and felt the depth of her breath. A wave of memories flooded with the power of an ocean. With the name of Allah on her lips, she closed her eyes.

Chapter Three

Diamond in the rough...

Death would have been easy to accept than the constant reminder of the losses in Abeedah's life. She had no idea how many hours had passed while she was lying dead on the rocks unconscious. She was still having some trouble to open her eyes. Even in this state, she could hear a crunching sound of footsteps on dry leaves.

Braving herself, with efforts she opened her eyelids in pain. All she saw was blurry images and instantly closed her eyes back again. The footsteps sounded closer and she opened her eyes once more focusing so she could see. She saw the silhouette of a large person standing above her. Forcing her eyes to focus more, she saw his intense eyes looking at her. A man in the possible dirtiest clothes if one could call them clothes dragged him inside the cave.

Under the moonlight, the clear vision was challenging, and a constant sound of hissing echoed all the directions. The cave smelled of mortuary and sawdust. Abeedah's vision started swimming again forcing her to shut her eyes and with a blink, her vision went dark. She was unconscious again.

The wind was heavy because of the dew. Abeedah felt the icy mist cold on the skin. The sunlight highlighted more colors during the day. She had been waiting for the morning for so long that she barely believed her eyes when the sharp shadows cast by the blackness, diluted by the onset of daylight.

Every inch of her body was mourning over Shad's and Ragini's death. She wanted to scream and cry out loud to release her pain, but her state was not supportive enough even to move an inch. One day she would mourn for him, but at first, she had to accept that Shad was no more. The neurons of her brain were grinding to a halt. She could now feel and hear everything around her but failed to provide a response to it.

Abeedah was traumatized, physically and mentally. After lying on the rocks for hours, she heard some crawling at a distance. She felt a pair of strong arms lifting her upper body and dragging her towards the sunlight. She could still hear the hissing but now, from a distance.

Abeedah felt the sensation of heat which started from her feet and reached her brain which made her heart, beat again. If not this moment, she would have never believed that God loved his children more than anything because he gave his most precious possession "The Sun."

Abeedah woke up with the sunlight on her face. The increase in the temperature of her body helped her in regaining the consciousness and gradually, she opened her eyes. Her whole body still hurt and it took her great effort to move her body and try to sit. For a fraction of a second, everything was calm. For a moment, she thought everything was a nightmare, and she will wake up on her soft bed. In the next minute, she realized that it was not a nightmare and neither was she lying on her soft bed.

It was a muddy ground covered with dry leaves and bushes. Somebody saved her from the state of being dead. Was it Siddhant? Who else could have saved her? Siddhant was missing throughout from the scene. She started looking for him, and with stumbling legs she went inside the caves.

It was a strange thirst like she had never experienced before. Her saliva was thick enough to lubricate her dryness. Her throat was dry like the skin had been extracted and laid out in the scorching sun. She thought of quenching her thirst from a nearby pond but she couldn't because bandits would have been still searching for her.

From a distance, she could hear a hissing sound. She assumed couple of snakes roaming around water. She had to get inside the cave in the search for water. As she was getting closer to the cave, it got darker, and the hissing got louder.

The cave was similar to a maze, but she figured out the way into it. She saw a pinch of sunlight reflecting upon a small water pond. The sunshine was like tiny dews spread over the ceiling of the cave. She stood there staring at the ceiling and completely forgot about the snakes which might be hiding near the water. It was too dark to even see her own footsteps but could see the reflections of that small pond.

With her unsteady steps, she reached the dugout and sat near the shallow water to quench her thirst. While making an attempt to drinking water from her small palm, someone lit the fire lamp. With the yellow fire light, she saw a shiny skin of black snake crossing over her shoes.

The vision got into her nerves, and she jumped back in all her intensity and fell on the ground. She looked around and realized that there were not one or two but dozens of snakes surround her. To her surprise, the snakes were not bothered with her presence in the cave.

At a distance, she saw some human resemblance. The slightest thought of a human company around, ignited her hope. She was confident that he was Siddhant. She was amazed with his survival instinct among these snakes. Slowly but gradually she followed that it wasn't him. He had a large body like Vikings with the similar savage appearance. It was easy to sense his condition from his aching voice, which seemed to be weak, injured.

Abeedah in her scared stammering voice "Hello, who are you?"

The strange man tried to stand unsteadily on his feet, and turned towards her, looking at him directly, she was petrified. The fear made her body forget to breathe. Her skin went cold and stunned. A giant shabby man with a stocky build, beard grown till the chest, and body covered with many wounds. Some appeared to be fresh, bleeding, while some were filled with pus. She thought he was a merciless ghost because it was nearly impossible for a human being to survive in this adverse condition with such unbearable wounds. She wondered, for how long he had been living with this condition?

Before she could inquire anything, the wounded man fainted and fell on the ground. After which, what she saw was no less than any miracle and hard to believe. The snakes gathered around him, and started biting all over his body. Abeedah could sense the intention of the snakes. They were not harming but helping him to recover from his pain. Their hissing sound was entirely different when they have intention of attacking someone. Its echo was distinct as if they were trying to wake him up.

Abeedah knew their venom were used for anesthesia and painkillers but when made synthetically. But it was beyond her understanding, how snake's venom can directly help a person to cure and if those snakes have achieved their intelligence or they were just helping a companion.

It was an unbelievable sight for her eyes. In fact, it was too much for her to handle it so quickly. She was undergoing a severe trauma yet tried to convince herself that all she saw was just her imagination; it was difficult for her to decide how to react to such situation or help that man. Instead she decided to run, without catching a breath, she ran towards the forest.

After running for few meters, she found herself under open sky in the middle of dense forest. Her conscious was feeling guilty that she had left him suffering in pain. She was feeling ashamed of herself being a doctor, above all being a human. She felt so small in front of those vertebrates, who are considered dangerous for life, were trying to save him. Their actions made them more human than her, making her feel like a coward. Also, Abeedah was not aware of the possible danger in the forest and it is said that a known risk is better than an unknown one. She decided to go back to the cave with her shivering steps.

This time, the snakes sensed Abeedah's intension and cleared path for her as she walked in. After sitting beside him for a while, she reached out to him. His body was hot as a condition of fever. With her medical skill she knew exactly what to do, she collected water on those steal mug, wet the piece of cloth she had and place it on his forehead, which was barely visible due to the long and uneven hair. She cleaned his wounds using her hijab.

Slowly, the cold water pulled his temperature down. It seemed like he was starving for ages and so was Abeedah. In the day light, she went out searching for some fruits and herbs. By afternoon, she had enough eatables in her pocket and hands to return to the cave. She sat quietly, tied her long hair and started mashing those fruit pulp and herbs together using the base of the steal mug, which was the only utensil around. The most challenging part was to feed him because of his terrifying feature. But he had to be fed for his recovery.

After feeding him and cleaning his other pair of clothes in the pond, all she needed was a peaceful rest. She arranged a place for sleep and slept within few minutes. It was pitch dark and cold by then. The only source of warmth was that small bonfire burning in the cave which lasted for a couple of hours.

Daylight was quite easy to pass but the night always brought a hidden fear beneath it shadow. Abeedah had seen nature's darkness before which creates an illusion of a street light into an old-fashioned film. This shade was nowhere similar to it. This time she had felt the treachery of darkness. It had robbed her of best possible senses and replaced it with a sense of paralyzed fear. After the fire released black smoke, everything went pitch black even the moon light looked for occasion to show itself, the only thing she felt was the presence of her eyes because she could feel herself blink. Her slumber got disturbed every time, she heard a strange sound around her. In this way, her night got carried away by keeping a check on the suffering man's condition.

Where the darkness felt infinite, daytime passed quickly in scavenging. It was as repeating cycle which was going on for many days. Days passed by, but no one came in search of her. On the other hand, the giant's wounds were taking all the time in the world to heal. She got used to the darkness by now.

One beautiful night, when the moon was utterly illuminated, scattering its light all over the sky and on the earth. It was peaceful. Far away from the chaotic world, where people are ready to kill each other in the name of religion, money, and power, this dense forest, cave, those snakes were her new world. It was difficult to survive, but this place had no fear, hate or suffering. A world for which Abeedah used to pray since her childhood days, but it came at the cost her close one's life.

Her Mamu always said, "Everything we wish for, from the core of our heart will be granted. But it comes with a price." He also said, "Sometimes what we get are not what we wish for, but it turns out to be what we need." He had views on every life situation. Copied or original nobody knew.

The surrounding was quiet, no news channel telecasting political rivalry, no terrorist attacks, nothing. She quietly sat in the corner. Her eyes, gazing the man, hoping that he will wake up from his long sleep. Though he looked like an ancient nomad, there was something peculiar about him and the way he was suffering, which could be deciphered from his face. His wounds were old and he had made peace with it. This cave was his home or maybe a temporary one.

Abeedah was sure that he was not a rational human being. Perhaps, he was an alien or some mutated human or may be suffering from a deadly virus destroying his body, and those snakes were his protectors. Numerous thoughts and theories were hovering her mind. She had never seen anyone or anything like this, in her life.

Whatever he was, Abeedah was sure of one thing that she wouldn't have been alive if it wasn't for him. He was the reason behind her survival. He kept her cautious the entire time as she had no idea of what he might turn out to be when he will gain his consciousness. He was her survival instinct, which gave her the right perspective to survive. He was her only company in disguise. It was he, who kept her aware and forced to structure her day precisely. It was her only job for the whole day which saved her from losing mind. She was too busy in keeping him alive, and it did not give her the time to dwell on the hopeless situation.

Days passed like a rapid fire questions, twenty-ninth days to be exact, of her survival, and yet nobody came to her rescue. Abeedah used to think about Siddhant, but with no clue, her thoughts never got any direction. Since last ten days, she hasn't heard of those bandits roaming around which meant they might have shifted their camp. The strange man was also recovering from his condition, his wounds were not bleeding anymore at least most of them.

Night before, he woke up for few minutes and asked for water and for next two days, he was conscious. She was worried about him. Although his wounds were recovering, she had no idea what to do next, if he doesn't wake up.

Chapter Four

Mi`raaj of the Believer.

One night, while Abeedah was dreaming of Shad and the time they had spent together at the camp. When her beautiful dream got interrupted by the sound of footsteps, she got terrified with a thought, if the bandits were back. In anxiety, she got up quickly and turned around to look for the ill man, but he was not there. Where was he? She was worried about him.

She blew off the bonfire and hid behind the dark waiting for those bandits to pass. This time, she was prepared to fight back if they catch her. The thought of losing her life did not mattered anymore. It was her time to take revenge for everything they took away from her.

On the other hand, she was scared for the safety of the stranger as well who was eventually the only familiar person around. Those bandits were brutal, feared engrossed through her thinking of what they could do to that poor sick person who wasn't even able to stand on his own. She overcame her fear and steadily searched for the man by following the crunching sound of the dry leaves.

To her surprise she saw him standing near a mango tree. She realized that it wasn't those bandit but his footsteps. He was targeting mangoes with the stones, and it was amazing to see him throwing those little pieces of stones without missing any target, even in such pitch dark.

This incidence reminded Abeedah of a mythical character she saw as a child in her school play about the famous battle of Mahabharata, Arjuna. The play was about his well known skill of aiming at a bird's eye. This man's actions and his personality also was no less than that of a warrior.

She rushed back to the cave to pretend she hasn't seen anything; also she didn't want him to find her spying over him. She turned towards the cave when she saw one of the snakes hissing at her. She stood still and was about to scream when a hand came from her back tightly shutting her mouth and pulled her back. It was the cave man, and they concealed themselves behind the bush. Those bandits were patrolling the forest area. They waited for them to pass and soon returned to the cave.

For the first time he was standing in front of her in his full strength. Too many questions were boggling up her mind to ask, but she couldn't utter a single word, and he also stood there silently. He lit up the fire and sat beside it. Abeedah sat at a distance figuring out the first question she wanted to ask him. Meanwhile, he took out the mangoes from his bag, he made himself. Distributing the fruits into two shares on small bowls made of leaves, siding one bowl towards her.

"My name is Abeedah. What is your name?" she broke the ice between them.

He looked at her. After giving an angry, serious look, he replied, "Abdus Samad."

"Great! You are a Muslim, too."

"I don't belong to any of the religion."

It was the boldest statement which Abeedah have heard in her lifetime. The rest of the night passed away in silence. Abeedah could not gather much of courage to talk to him. The very next day, she woke up with a loud noise of a helicopter passing by somewhere close. Without wasting any time, she ran outside the cave and shouted "Help! Help! Here! Here!" Her voice was not audible enough for the pilot to get his attention. She gathered a pile of dry leaves lying on the ground and ignited fire on it. The white fumes caught an attention of the pilot.

Unfortunately, that pilot was not the only one who caught a glimpse of those white fumes. Within a blink of an eye, four men with surrounded Abeedah with their guns pointed at her. Their eyes showed their clear intension of wanting to kill Abeedah. Their guns were black with a short snout with an uneven stock. One of them curled his finger around the trigger and smiled grimly at her. The other bandit wearing a gold bracelet reached behind him and took his gun out. He ensured that his gun was fully loaded. She closed her eyes in fear. She thought how many times she can dodge her death.

It was inevitable, but the universe had some other plans for her. It was not her time to die. One by one, all three of those bandits fell because of the stone was thrown at them. She turned back and saw the cave man throwing the fourth rock on the fourth one. No sooner the stone hit that bandit's head, and he fired a bullet in panic at him which pierced his shoulder.

Then she saw the helicopter hovering in the air right above her head, painted in red and yellow, light, single-engine aircraft. A glimpse of a figure in dark glasses and helmet hunched over the controls was visible. The blades were beating the air very swiftly. The red, green paint enveloped in a cloud of sandy dust.

The blades had somewhat the same effect what a small tornado can do on a loose ground cover. Slowly it landed, Abeedah covered her ears because of the loud noise of its blade It was the rescue team who used to conduct their patrolling whenever needed in that area. Luckily, they heard the gunshot and came for her help. Abeedah felt responsible for the cave man's injury. Those bandits could have taken his life. What if their bullet would have pierced his chest? All these thoughts made her heart beat super-fast, and tears were rolling down her eyes.

One of the officers said "Ma'am, My name is Abhinav. Please don't worry. We won't let anything happen to you and him."

Abhinav informed the local hospital for an emergency operation via his cordless connected to a control room,

"Ma'am, your name please?" Abhinav asked.

She replied in a slow and stammering voice "Abeedah.. My name is Abeedah Hassan."

"Ma'am, may I know the patient's name?"

"Abdus Samad," The two officers along with Abeedah carried Abdus into the helicopter, he was too heavy for a person. The flow was heavy and he had lost a lot of blood which made his condition serious. They flew away from the forest and reached hospital in no time.

Abdus's operation went on for six hours. Sitting on the iron chair, outside the operation theatre, Abeedah was blaming herself for everything that had happened. She covered her face with her palm and started weeping. After some time she heard the melodious sound of azaan in the air. She had a long and a dreadful day. She was all tired, and her body was aching.

One might think that it is difficult for a restless person to concentrate on her prayers to God, the Almighty. Snuggled up in a warm and cozy bed, how difficult it is to get up at the call of prayer.

Prophet Mohammad once said, "The prayer is the Mi`raaj of the Believer."

Abeedah stood up from her waiting chair and prepared for Salah, an obligatory form of worshipping in Muslims by bowing down while praying.

She cleaned herself with the tap water. Although her clothes were quite dirty, she had a clean heart. She calmed herself from those worldly thoughts and worries. She sat in the hallway corner and prayed to Allah. After completing the second rakat, a unit of an Islamic prayer consisting of certain words and movements. A teardrop fell from her eyes to reaching her chin.

After her prayer, she asked Allah "Why all my loved ones always end up dead, leaving me alone? My Ammi (mother) died while giving birth to me. I don't know anything about my father, apart from the fact that he died when I was three years old. My beloved Shad and my best friend Ragini were paid the cost for my happiness. And now Abdus? He was in a better before I met him. At least he was alive, and now his life is in danger. I pray to you for his health. Please save him.

Bless him with your grace."

She had a firm belief that the Almighty would not let him die. By the time she came back after her prayer, the operation was over, and Abdus was out of the Operation Theater but the doctors didn't let her see him. Doctors were confused about Abdus's health. They had a strange feedback about him, but they haven't revealed anything clear to Abeedah about his condition. She felt suspicious and followed a doctor who was holding his reports. She heard them talking about his status.

"His cells are behaving abnormally, unlike any other human being. It is because of these cells his ageing is prolonged as compared to any one of us. This kind of mutation is beyond our scientific and logical understanding!"

It was a unique case for them in their history of the practice. Doctors wanted to perform some more tests on him. They called up different experts from all over the country and tightened the security around him. Being a doctor herself, Abeedah understood their concealed intention behind such tests. She knew that they would be using him as a guinea pig for their research and experiments. For them, Abdus was no more than a test subject to explore their mystery. Abdus was not safe, but it was tough for Abeedah to save him.

Abeedah was experiencing tremendous stress. Her mouth got as dry as a sandbox in the summer. Every moment passed by leading to the next one. The situation was so fragile that her heart was racing against her ribcage like a geared bullet. No-one spoke about Abdus, what was there to say? If anything happens to him, it will be Abeedah who would be needing medication and treatment.

She had already crossed her threshold of tolerating terrible situations, and anything wrong goes by, this time she would break down. She could feel the fear in her chest taking control of her. It was right there like an angry ball pushing her towards a state of anxiety. She was pacing back and forth in the hallway, figuring out a way to get Abdus out of the hospital. When she couldn't think straight, she went out for some fresh air.

There she saw a little string of hope, Abhinav, from the rescue team, at a distance heading towards the chopper. He was her only hope who could have helped her in saving Abdus. She was not sure, but her body started feeling relaxed after seeing a familiar face. She ran toward him, calling him by his name, again and again.

"Abhinav! Mr. Abhinav!"

He stopped and turned back, "Yes ma'am, you seem to be worried. How may I help you?"

"Mr. Abhinav — "

"Ma'am, please call me Abhinav." He interrupted.

Stress was on her face, but with a smile, she explained him the situation. She begged him for help. "Please help me. Abdus is not safe here. Doctors are conducting some experimental tests on him.

Please help me in getting him out of here. I would be very grateful to you, Abhinav."

"Ma'am..ma'am. Please slow down. Take a deep breath and tell me how I can help you.", Abhinav replied with a concern on his face.

After explaining him the plan to save Abdus, he agreed and asked her to meet at the backside lamp post by midnight. Now, the only thing she needed was some cash for their travel and food. It was going to be a long journey to home. She arranged some money against whatever jewelry she had on her, but it was not enough. Then she looked at the beautiful diamond ring on her finger. It was her engagement ring.

Looking at the ring took her back to the day when Ragini and Siddhant were getting engaged. Everything around her was beautiful. She could feel the freshness and fragrance of tulips decorated on the side of the stairs. She looked at Shad, and she knew that he was the one she was supposed to spend her whole life with but things don't go as planned, this is life. After Ragini and Siddhant got engaged, Siddhant called Shad on the stage for a surprise performance. It was supposed to be a massive surprise for Abeedah.

Keeping aside Shad's good looks, he was undoubtedly a terrible performer. Abeedah, no matter what, always cheered him up. After Shad's performance, he called up her name out of the blue. Ragini pushed hers from behind to move her feet. While she walked onto the stage, she saw a ring on Shad's hand and in that moment, she realized, what was coming. Shad proposed her with this beautiful diamond ring. It was all a setup.

The moment she was taking it off her finger, she knew she was giving up her last memory with Shad. She knew that she was letting him go from her life. She sold the ring to save someone's life. Of all the emotions, Abeedah knew the value of life and no other emotion could have stopped her from selling her engagement ring.

All together she had 60,000 rupees in her pocket now; she went back to the hospital and waited for Abhinav at the exact same spot he had asked her to meet. From the back door, she saw Abhinav dragging a body in a wheelchair. He was Abdus. This view brought a smile on her face for which she couldn't thank Abhinav enough. But, she couldn't ignore the expressions of Abhinav face too.

Finally, he asked, "Ma'am, if you don't mind, who he is? Why are you protecting him to this extent? I'm sorry, but I couldn't help it noticing that he doesn't seem like a normal man and anyway related to you."

Abeedah kept her silence for a while then staring at Abdus's face, she replied

"He is a friend. Who saved my life. So, now it is my responsibility to save his life."

Abeedah was equally curious to ask him one question. "How did you manage to get him out here?"

"I exchanged his body with a body from the morgue. Though it was challenging to find a body which could match his huge structure, it was close enough. And disguise is one thing we are trained to be." He smiled. "This is the last one I can help you with, here. My disappearance will question my involvement in this. I need to go immediately."

Getting Abhinav falling into any trouble was the last thing Abeedah ever wanted. So, with regards, she went on her way with Abdus and disappeared into the smogy chill of that night.

Chapter Five

Faith! Right?

Abeedah was aware of this fact that her journey would be arduous hence onwards. She was walking in the middle of the night, and such thoughts were making her feel tense. Till now, the hospital authorities would have known this fact that Abdus was missing. Moving around openly with him was not safe anymore, but there was no other option as well. She realised that she could not check into any hotel because they did not have any identity proof. The city was small yet had essence of calmness in it.

With God's grace, her eyes fell on a board in front of a house which was open for renting out. She knocked the door with hope. After couple of minutes, an old lady answered the door. She had a fair skin with a stern face. Her cheeks were all wrinkled, and they were sagging till her mid neck. Half grey and half white hair gave her a close resemblance with Cruella de-vil so do her expression. She had an annoyed expression on her face because her sleep got disturbed by Abeedah's knock. It was by hook or crook, Abeedah had to convince this old lady for granting her shelter.

"Hello ma'am, my na—"Abeedah said in a hesitant voice.

The old lady interrupted her in between and asked in a gruff voice "What do you want?"

"Ma'am, my name is Abeedah, and this is my friend, Abdus. He is very sick, and we are looking for a place to stay for a few days."

"So, what can I do?" the old lady's irritation grew worse.

"Ma'am, there is a 'for rent' sign at your door. So…" Abeedah shrugged her shoulder as a gesture that she had completed her answer to that lady's question.

"Ooh! I forgot! For how many months do you want?"

"Only for few days or so. My friend went through an operation, and as soon as he recovers, we will leave. We are from Mumbai and…." She got interrupted again by that old lady.

The old lady, "Sorry, I can't help you. I am looking for a long-term tenant. Look I am old and an alone 'girl' who got to eat." Abeedah tried really hard not to roll her eyes on the fact that an old lady was referring herself being a girl. She wanted to laugh out loud and thought that this lady needs a mirror in her house or she might have lost the pace of time. She was not a girl, not even a middle-aged woman. She was an old and wrinkled lady.

"Don't worry about it. I will pay you for a whole month." Abeedah ensured that lady with all her convincing skills.

"Okay! You can stay. But I have some rules, and everyone will have to follow it. I don't care what kind of relationship you two are having. I don't want any disturbance in my house, especially at night. You will have to keep your space clean, and I am very strict about it. No guests allowed and the food is entirely your responsibility. Am I clear?"

"Yes ma'am that would not be an issue." Abeedah nodded with a deep sigh.

It was a comfortable two bedroom house connected to the hall and kitchen. Both separated by a five seated dining table. The furniture was quite old fashioned, and the plaster was falling from the ceiling and walls because of the layers of paint. Some of the tiles were missing from the floor while some were cracked. The lower part of the door was majorly affected by the termites, and the curtains looked shabby. Still, the place was clean as there was no sign of dust on the furniture.

"Okay, the left room is mine. You can take the right one, it's spacious!" said the old lady in a casual tone.

Abeedah nodded and pushed Abdus's wheelchair towards the room when she heard knock on the table, twice. She murmured "Now what! You old grumpy lady..." and turned back.

"Money first,"

"Sure, ma'am" Abeedah sighed.

By the time Abeedah was counting the required rent, the old lady was staring at Abdus's face. She said in a gruff voice "By the way, this is not Mumbai. I don't how why today's generation want this bearded look. In our days, clean shaved man with a moustache was called a gentleman."

Abeedah paid her the rent and noticed the happiness for money on the lady's face. Indeed, it was a stressful day, but Abeedah had made it. She was worried for Abdus because he was still unconscious because of the blood lost. His skin looked pale and need time to recover. But who how long he will take to walk and talk and if he didn't wake up soon, she had no idea what she would do.

Abeedah went to the room and cleaned Abdus's body with a wet towel and slowly pulled him to the bed. She found a couch for herself to lie down and rest.

After banging her head the whole day, staring at the ceiling, she felt the calmness which she used to experience in the forest. She missed watching that skyline full of stars and waking up with the sun rays on her face which was now replaced with the old ceiling and slow moving blades of fan. She craved the touch of the cool breeze on her head and smell of the soil. With such thoughts, her eyes felt heaviness, and she fell asleep in no time.

The very next morning, she woke up early to get some medicines and food. She ran to the market got stumbled by her childhood memories. There were small shops with colourful banners on all the sides of the road. Children were playing on the street with a bicycle tire, rolling them. People were greeting and wishing each other. Happy faces living a peaceful life. Even the charming environment couldn't escape from the clutches of evil. few hundred meters away from the medical store, the whole place torn apart

Abeedah asked the shopkeeper "Kaka, what happened there?"

He replied, "That place used to be a great neighbourhood. Couple of days back, bandits came for their monthly fee—"

She interrupted "Fees? For what?"

He replied "Fees… for sparing our lives" sadness could be seen in his eyes.

"What happened then?" she asked anxiously.

"When we had nothing to offer them neither money nor any crop, they burned our houses, killed men and took their wives and children with them."

The act was horrendous, but she was not much surprised by it. Such incidents were making people accustomed to it in the world. She sympathised with the shopkeeper and could feel his pain. Around a month back, she had also undergone the same pain. She picked up the supplies in a cotton bag and went towards her temporary home.

On her way back, she saw a barber shop. She thought something for a while and asked one of the barbers to come along with her. Anxiously, she drove Abdus in his wheelchair in the sunlight and asked the barber to shave his beard and trim his hair and asked her to help her clean him up. By the time she cleaned her room and came back, she saw something she never expected.

Abdus turned out to be the most handsome man she could have ever seen. Abeedah has seen his eyes but now with a shave, his features and strong jawline were more pronounced making his face very attractive. His eyes closed framed by long lashes and bushy brows. He had a straight nose which was bent slightly in the middle as if it was broken at some point and never healed properly. His full wide lips and dimpled chin completed his look complimenting his dusky skin tone . His inky black hair was cut short in sides and was left in a wavy mess on the top. A lock of hair partially covered a deep and old scar on his forehead which was surprisingly still bleed continuously. It was difficult to think of an adequate reason for the occurrence of such injury. It was always a mystery for Abeedah as exactly what was Abdus up to in those thick forests? He was truly a diamond in the rough.

Days passed, but Abdus' condition was constant. In this while, Abeedah her connection with Mrs. Gaikwad, the old lady. She was not as grumpy as Abeedah thought, just old.

One night while cooking dinner Mrs. Gaikwad asked her, "Abeedah, what happened? Anything bothering you?"

"No aunty, I am fine," Abeedah said in a low voice.

"Don't you worry my dear, your friend will wake up soon from his sleep. Just have faith."

In the background a female voice on the television was announcing breaking news, "Another terrorist attack in the USA. This is the fifth attack of this year. A gunman has opened fire in a school and has killed and hurt more than 50 people including children and teachers and staff of the school. Reports are coming in that the perpetrator has been shot down by the snipers as he was refusing to cooperate in the hostage negotiations and as last resort he had been taken down. The perpetrator has been identified as Michael Keifer and he has a history of domestic abuse and violence. This again brings up the debate about the need of amendment of gun control laws in America. In the mean time the prayers are coming from all over the world with strong condemning of the incident. We pray that the victims come out safe and strong after this and have faith in god."

"Faith! Right?" Abeedah said in a sarcastic tone after hearing the news.

Mrs. Gaikwad, while peeling off some potatoes said in a very soft tone, "Honey, God works mysteriously. We tend to lose hope because of the current situation irrespective of the fact that we have no idea about the occurrence of our future. The universe listens to your wishes, and it is completely upon him how and in what way your wish is granted.

We all pay the price in exchange for what we get. I am not asking you to be optimistic, but you can uphold the faith. It's in your hands, right?" She widened her eyes towards Abeedah for the positive feedback.

"Well, that's what my husband used to say before leaving me alone in this world.", Mrs. Gaikwad sighed.

Her words were not new for Abeedah. She had already read it in some books. The old lady's words helped her in recalling them. It did assist her in igniting a ray of hope inside her.

"Do you have any children Mrs. Gaikwad?" she asked with a twisted smile.

"Three, actually. Two sons and a daughter," she replied.

"Really? Then why do you stay alone?" she asked suspiciously.

"Well, they all wanted to transform me and my habits. I believe it is impossible to change someone's lifestyle which had been practicing it for 70 years. " Mrs. Gaikwad smelled the spices from the curry by waving her hand from the pot to her nose.

Abeedah felt pity for her. Giving her a side look, Mrs. Gaikwad said, "There is nothing to feel pity for me. When they were kids, I taught them to live as per my rules, and when they grew up, it was their turn to frame new rules which I never obeyed. You know, I was never an obedient child." She laughed a little just to hide her tears.

"So they don't visit you?"

"Initially? Every week. Slowly week converted into months and then into occasions. Being busy is the most common excuse, and it doesn't leave with much of an option to argue." Her voice desolated.

"Don't you feel sad and alone?" Abeedah asked.

"Well, people call a husband and wife each other's soul mate for a reason! Irrespective of how annoying they are to each other, they are deeply rooted emotionally, especially at our age. After living so many years together, if one can learn to live without their better half, everything becomes bearable. I believe losing your soul mate is an ultimate pain for anyone."

After a long pause, she continued, "Living without a partner is that one thing which you can never get habitual to it. I wish it never happens to you". She smiled at Abeedah as if showering all her blessings.

Her blessings were not more than an irony for Abeedah. She hasn't disclosed her past, but she understood what Mrs. Gaikwad was experiencing. They both were sailing in the same boat, unknowingly. Abeedah chuckled softly and said, "I should check on Abdus now. Its time to change his bandage." After all she had no idea how to console the poor woman when she had trouble consoling herself.

Chapter Six

God favors injustice?

O ne lousy evening, while pulling out the syringe from his veins, Abeedah felt his fingers moving. She did not think much about it, and she started changing his bandages. She felt that it was her imagination. While applying an ointment on his body, all of a sudden, he woke up and grabbed her wrist very tightly, stopping her from touching him.

"Where am I? What am I doing here? Why have you brought me here?" Abdus asked furiously without pausing in between of his questions.

She could see the anger in his eyes which scared her to death. His eyes were wild and intense that Abeedah was at loss of words to answer his question. He left her wrist after seeing her face turning pale out of fear. He pulled off that syringe from his other hand and jumped off the bed.

She tried to calm down, "Hey! Hey! I am Abeedah. I am the girl from the cave, remember? You were shot, and I had to take you to a hospital, and you went somewhat into a state of coma..."

He looked at her wide eyed as if she was had grown two more heads. He shouted, "What are you saying?"

Abeedah doubted if Abdus was hit on the head and suffering from partial amnesia? What kind of question was that?

"Abeedah, What is happening there, what is that noise?" Mrs. Gaikwad shouted from the kitchen.

Hearing her voice, Abdus ran towards the hall, and Abeedah followed him. He saw Mrs. Gaikwad holding the pot of curry. She was shocked and was about to drop that pan. It was not because she saw Abdus in all his senses but because of his physical appearance.

A thirty something old man, oddly 7 feet tall, with a broad chest and muscular arms was standing in front of her. His palms were so big that it could cover an infant easily. She had always seen him wrapped in a blanket, slouched and his stature was too much to for an old lady to digest.

She was afraid, which was evident his her stammering as she finally asked

"Oh finally… you are awake!" she was unable to take her eyes off of him. It took her some time to recover when she realised that he wont hurt them. She recovered and asked her in a strong voice.

"How are you feeling now? Sit. Have your dinner." For the first time, Abeedah noticed Mrs. Gaikwad motherly affection towards Abdus.

His anger cooled off within a second. It was strange. He stood there frozen for several minutes his eyes moving rapidly taking notes of his surrounding. Both the women were scared of his reaction and stood without saying anything. After sometime they saw the man relax and finally realise that he was safe. He pulled back a chair and sat on it. Abeedah was surprised to see this sudden change in his mood. She also sat next to his chair. Mrs. Gaikwad served him some rice with curry and homemade pickles. Without waiting for the next moment, he attacked his meal just like a lion strikes his target. It seemed like as if he was eating food for the first time.

It was amusing watching an overgrown man, eating like a child. Mrs. Gaikwad and Abeedah looked at each other biting their lips to hold their laugh. "Do you want more?" Mrs. Gaikwad patted her gently on his head.

He looked at her motherly face and nodded positively. After completing three additional servings, he washed his hand and without uttering a word, he went back to the room. Abeedah apologised to Mrs. Gaikwad for his strange behaviour and followed him back. She noticed his worry and murmurs. He was pacing back and forth in the room. "I can't be here. I can't stay with them! I have to go back to the forest."

Abeedah tried to pull his hand which was too big for her to hold. "What are you so afraid of, who the hell are you? I am trying to help you out, and you are not even grateful!"

She had developed an intense bond after staying with him for these many days. She felt a weird sense of right upon him. The truth was she genuinely cared for him which he was not aware of. He got irritated and pulled off his hand angrily, "You shouldn't have brought me here..."

"Do you have any idea how sick you are? How much medical attention you need?" she asked incredulously.

"You can't do anything about it. They are eternal. They will never heal. You understand? Just leave me alone if you want to stay alive!" He said apprehensively.

"Oh really? If your wounds are eternal, then how come they are healing? And what do you mean by want to stay alive?" she asked, one eyebrow raised.

"That is impossible—" He looked all over his body. He checked his arms and his chest. All He looked up and saw a mirror on the wall. He went up and saw that the wounds on his face one the verge of healing though the wound on his forehead was still bleeding.

"How is this happening? They are not bleeding anymore!" He looked at Abeedah with all his happiness.

She was still angry because her questions were unanswered. She repeated, "WHO ARE YOU?"

"I am nobody. Not required for you to know." He replied arrogantly and laid down on the bed.

Abeedah was having whiplash from his hot and cold attitude. She turned and left the room. Maybe he needs some time to himself. But how long? He had all his time in that forest! She was confused, but she was sure enough that neither he was not an ordinary human, nor was he sick. He had a storm of secrets hidden inside him, but she had no clue how to help him further.

She lied down on the couch and closed his eyes. His calm and mysterious face dancing behind her eyes. She thought if it right to ask him to stay when he didn't want to? He saved her life for she saved his, showing her gratitude to him. He is now conscious enough to walk on his own chosen path, but deep down Abeedah didn't want to let him go… he was that beam of light which gave her a reason to wake up every morning. Otherwise, her life was now full of darkness.

For Abeedah his silence conveyed a strong message. She exactly knew why silence is a golden practice because she believed, silence is the best answer if you are misunderstood, ignored, avoided, ditched, hurt by anyone. If you go silent, that doesn't mean you are wrong. Sometimes it means you are strong. Sometimes it means you have the ability to understand and adjust with anyone at any situation. Sometimes it means you are maintaining your self respect and dignity. Sometimes it means you are deeply hurt. Sometimes it means you are disheartened. Sometimes it means you are highly disappointed and fed up with what you got from life. Sometimes it means you are done fighting for your rights. Sometimes it means you are better alone than having people around who do not have the heart to understand you, who don't give you respect and hurt you.

Silence is a Freedom for those who are not understood. It is better to be silent when you are misunderstood always. When your feelings are not accepted and understood by people, silence is the best in a long run. If people have the heart to understand, they will, even if you don't express. Abdus's silence could depict lots of reasons, behind it and Abeedah wasn't able to pick up a reason in her sane mind because it now, she wasn't his confidant.

At midnight, she woke up to some sound at the door. She woke up and found that Abdus was missing from his bed. Abeedah ran towards the door and looked outside from the window. He was going away. She wanted to call him, but something stopped her. She went to her room.

After few minutes, she heard the same sound at the door, but it was much louder. She ran towards the door happily thinking that Abdus was back. The next view gave her chills after seeing a group of men and women in the hall. They were breaking the furniture and tapping the floor very hard. Their rifles made a crackling and scratching sound on the floor. No sooner she saw them, she sneaked back into her room and hid inside a cabinet.

Mrs. Gaikwad, unaware of the upcoming danger, came out of her room calling for Abeedah. Hearing her voice, Abeedah jumped out of the wardrobe. Before she could help her out, one of the men in a half burnt face, aimed her. He fired, and the bullet passed through somewhere near her chest. Within a second, she fell on the floor. She screamed furiously with tears shredding her eyes. She tried to hit him but quickly, he caught her by placing a knife on her neck. He inquired for Abdus.

"Where is he?"

"Who?" she asked in an almost inaudible voice.

"That tall man, who had killed our brothers." He asked.

"Kill me… I will tell you nothing. You swine!" she cried.

"Fine. Your wish is my command, your highness!" he replied sarcastically and started pressing that knife against her neck. Her blood grew thicker and flowed in excess from her neck's skin. With each tick of the clock she wanted her heartbeat to stop, just stop. She closed her eyes to and waited for her life to end.

It wasn't her time to die. The room got covered with black smoke. Slowly, she opened her eyes, and with a slight shimmer, she saw two men like structures wearing a black cloak. A cloak probably made up of smoke. She was unable to see their faces, but they were holding an engraved sickle. The head was the shinny sickle like structure or half broken circle standing on a long stick inscribed with all sorts of mythical languages and symbols.

They were not human, and they were something like a phantom. Abeedah was confused whether she was experiencing a nightmare or reality. They were terrifying to look at directly. The furniture and the wall that peeled off because of the rising damp became slightly out of focus, like a blurred snap.

For a moment, everything was silent. Even the ticking of that antique clock on the wall. The room was melting. It was boiling as if everyone has gone to hell, like literally a hell. They did not have their feet. They almost float in the air and stood side by side. They joined their stick, and the sickle was now a complete circle.

The carved scripts and symbols started glowing like a fire and one by one it started sucking the soul of everyone present in the hall. In front of her eyes, they acquired everyone's soul. No sooner the soul was being extracted the bodies of those men and women started falling on the floor. Dead was a trivial word.

Something else was happening. They even took away Mrs. Gaikwad soul too. They were Reapers. Soon, they vanished into thin air but left with an echo, "Go, get him."

Abeedah was watching from a small hole in that cabinet. She fell on my knees and sat there for some time. She was unable to gulp that sight. She waited under the veil of black for a moment. She couldn't breathe. She felt choked. Her heart was pounding and all she to get curled up into a ball. She wanted and waited for someone to save her. She realised that no one could save her. She was all alone. Abdus was no more there to protect her. Abeedah pulled herself and ran after Abdus. She started following his footprints which were no wonder of considerable size. She was panicking and looked for Abdus like a mad woman roaming on the street. After few hours of searching, she got into an isolated area.

She found him sitting under a tree, in front of a bonfire. His sight calmed her nerves. She went up to him and sat beside him. Her throat was as dry as a desert, but she could feel her thirst getting quenched just by Abdus's presence.

"Please don't leave. Those people killed Mrs. Gaikwad." She said with a drop running down her cheek. Abdus didn't respond. He sat quietly near the bonfire. The temperature had fallen more in the atmosphere.

Abeedah cried, and she slept near the bonfire, sobbing. Early morning she woke up and saw the white smoke flaring out of an extinguished fire. She looked for Abdus. He was nowhere. He had left her, again! She sat in despair cursing herself for trusting Abdus. He was and is a stranger. In spite of living with him for more than a month, he was still a stranger. She felt a dead end at that moment. There was nothing left except to cry and cry.

She heard his voice. "If you want to cry all the time, you need to eat something. It will give you energy for crying." He came with some fruits and coconut water.

She looked at him and laughed at his comment. She took the coconut water from his hand and started drinking. While she was drinking, she saw a little stretching of some muscles at the corners of his lips. For the first time, he was smiling, maybe!

She looked at his brand new weird outfit. "New clothes... aren't they a little short for you? From where have you got it?

He replied in a humble tone, "I have spent most of my life in the forest inside the cave. Occasionally, I used to go for scavenging. There, I used to follow people who came to the forest. I don't know why people used to come in a group. So I collect whatever they used to leave behind."

"How long have you been in that forest?" Abeedah asked curiously.

"Too long. I am unable to recall my count."

"But tell me….Who are you and how did you get these wounds?"

His silence answered all her questions. His personality reflected some secrets which he was not comfortable to share, at least, not now. Therefore, she decided that she won't bother him by asking this question again. She had a gut feeling that all these weird incidents which she experienced were directly or indirectly connected to him. They decided it would be better if they went back to Mrs. Gaikwad's home. It felt insulting somehow when they entered the house as the owner herself was dead because of them but they were alive.

Next morning, both of them woke up to the sound of a bomb blast. They knew it was them, the bandits. Multiple bombings were happening at once all around the town. They had to find a way out from that place and reach to the nearest railway station. They ran for their lives. After several hours of running and hiding, Abeedah found a road which would lead them out of the town.

Vehicles were running down the road. She noticed Abdus getting uncomfortable around the crowd of people at once after a long time. Abeedah waved her hands on the roadside, to seek for a lift for hours. Finally, a truck loaded with vegetables stopped.

After offering him some money, he agreed to give them a lift to Nagpur check post. They happily jumped over the truck. Throughout their journey, she was noticing a pleasant glow on his face as if a bird released from a self-made cage. He was innocent to this cruel world.

He used to check his wounds now and then. It was unbelievable to him that his wounds were healing. It was evening, and Abeedah loved to see the sunset. After a long time, her wish was getting fulfilled but sadly, of so many lives. Her Mamu and Mrs. Gaikwad were right.

The whole sky was covered in different shades of red as if the sky was bleeding. The clouds were trying to hide its madness. The sun turned into orange in colour and left an impression of a happy ending. It was after ages she saw a soothing sunset and this one gave her an image of nature's anger and dragon fire. Suddenly, the truck stopped with a jerk. Abeedah peeped outside and saw some of the officers checking all the vehicles. They were inspecting as well as showing them a sketch of someone. She hid again and closed her eyes for better concentration. Then she heard his truck driver talking to a man.

"What are they checking for, another arms loaded truck?"

Other man said, "No. This time they are searching for a man. Apparently he is weird some seven feet tall and looks like a nomad or something."

It was Abdus. They were searching for Abdus. She forcibly patted Abdus's arms to wake him up. He always had a deep slumber. She told him furiously, "Wake up! Police is searching for you. We need to go immediately."

He squinted his eyes, "Police? What Police? Why?"

"Police are the ones who take criminals to the prison, real handsome hunky men….", she trailed, when she saw him smiling, realising he was not asking what cops were.

She sighed, "Long story short, we need to run. Fast! Before they could catch us."

The truck was at the Chhattisgarh-Maharashtra border. They jumped off the truck when it was standing in a queue for Police checking. Without getting caught, they ran towards the forest. Abeedah helped Abdus as he was staggering and seemed tired. Soon they found another road. They started walking along the road and ensured that no one was noticing them.

After walking for a few kilometres, they finally reached a Dhaba where several truck drivers were resting and having lunch. Both of them were hungry. She looked for money in her pocket and asked Abdus to hide behind the tree. It was difficult for her to ignore the glances of people on her because of her shabby appearance. She waited for her order and looked around for a minute. She noticed a truck was standing near that local food court, which was going to Mumbai. She couldn't believe her luck and in haste collected her food and a bottle of water.

Excited, she came back to Abdus. He was apparently taking a short nap and slowly opened his eyes when he heard her voice.

"Are you okay? Here, have some food." She sat in front of him and opened the parcel. Food never failed to make Abdus happy. After unwrapping the packing, he started gulping it swiftly. She couldn't help herself from smiling at Abdus's action.

Abeedah made a puking face when she saw a dead insect inside her food packet. Abdus casually removed the insect and started eating. She gave an unpleasant look to him.

"What? I have seen worst days! This food is way better than what I used to have in that forest." he said while eating.

Abeedah realised her mistake. She also felt sad for Abdus. He was a gentle person at heart and was the one to save her. In this world, he was all alone all this while. Her heart ached to ask him about his life, but she refrained herself from repeating the same mistake.

"Well, I have some good news. I have found a truck that is leaving for Mumbai."

"Mumbai? What is that?" He gave her a perplexed look.

"You don't know Mumbai? Bombay? You don't know?" Huh. Was he an early man? Then she felt stupid of her because he was living in a rock cave. Since when? God knows.

He nodded, "I know Bombay. They call it Mumbai now?"

"Yes, It's a really big city now." , she explained, thankful that he atlas knows Bombay. It won't be really hard for him to explain the city. He was still looked confused but nodded clearly not interested in the conversation anymore.

They had their food and waited for the truck driver to begin his journey. Somehow they managed to get themselves on the truck, and there started their longest and the most uncomfortable ride to their destination. Abeedah prayed to God for no more of any unforeseen surprises. They had enough surprises to last a week.

Abdus was a reserved man and a reticent person. With him, Abeedah had never felt so safe and protected ever in her life. It was not because of his size but because of the aura of his presence. He was already leading a stressful life yet he honoured her with emotional and physical security.

The days spent with him, precisely months, were the most difficult ones of her life which had transformed her completely. She was now a new person who had learned the art of overcoming extreme situations which she never believed before that she could ever do it.

They passed their journey by admiring the beauty of nature and breaking the ice between them by asking silly questions like:

"What is your favourite fruit?" or "Do you like papaya?" which Abeedah hated with an intensity. The question flowed between them, more from Abeedah than Abdus who mostly kept smirking while she talked.

At one point of time, she called him "Shad" and awkwardly stopped her conversation.

"Who is Shad?" Abdus asked.

"He was my fiancé."

Abdus asked, "Was?"

She replied mournfully, "Yes. Those bandits killed him in the forest."

Abdus had a indifferent on his face. Abeedah felt annoyed and said,"What? Have you ever heard of the word 'Empathy'? Do you know what is the feeling of losing someone special in your life or you have forgotten everything while living in that cave?"

He got irritated, long with hurt clear on his face, "Yes! Maybe I have been living for so long in the cave that I had lost my touch from life, or I have lost so many people close to me, that don't feel sad anymore."

Abeedah felt ashamed of her statement. She was still unaware of his past. "I am very sorry. I can understand your pain. My mother passed away while giving birth and my father died in an accident."

Abdus sighed, apparently deciding that it was not worth getting agitated, "I am sorry for your parents, and thank you for your sympathy. But you can't actually understand my pain. And I'm glad that you don't have to. I am no saying your pain is not valid, Abeedah, please don't think like that but no, you don't understand the my pain. In fact, you can't ever. At least it was an accident and not murder…." He paused. He was in pain because the memories of his past were haunting him.

Abeedah was stunned. She asked fearfully "Your parents were murdered?"

Abdus, "My father. He was tricked and murdered."

"By whom?"

"His students, my father taught them everything and in return, do you know what he got? Betrayal."

"Your father was a teacher?" She asked.

Abdus nodded.

"What happened then, those murderers were not caught or punished?"

Abdus chuckled, "If God is himself favouring injustice and is biased enough... the laws of nature forget its rules and frame its ways as per His wish. No one has any say in front of Him."

She had no idea what to say to that, so instead she asked, "And the other members of your family?"

"I have never seen my mother after my father's death. I had an uncle who had left me because of my one stupid move which I once made influenced by anger to avenge my father's death." he said in a heartbreaking tone.

There was nothing left to ask further that could have eased his pain. Slowly, she held his hand and with a consoling smile gazed at him. His story was sad, but she was happy that at last, he was coming out of his cocoon. The moonlight was dazzling on their head. It was all dark. They did not have any other option in the truck but to rest and live in nostalgia.

It was difficult to relax on a moving and jerky iron floor, but somehow between those jerks and iron cracking the skull, they drifted to sleep. After some time, she saw those reapers again. They were trying to follow and spy on them. She could not believe and thought that whether she was dreaming. She was unable to figure anything fruitful, and this made her uneasy. She felt goosebumps on the back of her neck. She was a night admirer, but such kind of visions elevated her wariness. She wanted the night to end and wake up soon to get over with such dream.

As the first glow of the sun touched her feet, she woke up and saw herself beside Abdus, her head resting on his unusually large palm. No wonder her nightmare vanished and she had a peaceful sleep. She looked at his face. His face was at peace whenever he used to sleep. Finally, that wound on his forehead had stopped bleeding as well. Was it him, who had positioned her head on his palm? She wondered whether he had this feeling of care for her.

Chapter Seven

This is bliss...

Abeedah felt cheerful as soon as she saw the green route map towards Mumbai. They have been travelling for more than twenty hours, periodically taking bathroom and meal breaks when the trucks stopped. As soon as they reach Mumbai, Abeedah inhaled a deep breath into her lungs. She felt a strange sort of enjoyment in feeling the air of her city. "This is my city!" she whispered.

In her excitement, she patted Abdus and informed "Wake up! We have reached our destination."

Abdus woke up and sat casually. His eyes were not gleaming as of Abeedah because of Mumbai, but he couldn't ignore the skylines and the rush of the city. Abeedah noticed his stare and understood his chaotic thoughts.

"The world has changed a lot since the last you have seen it!" she smiled.

"You can't even imagine..." He was still staring at skyscrapers with his eyes wide open.

Abeedah forgot that Abdus was wearing bizarre clothes. His pants were short enough for his legs, and he was covering his broad chest with a multicolour scarf having multiple nodes. The truck dropped them in Dadar.

Abeedah, standing in the middle of the road, "Oh! I missed this sound of the horns buzzing around and the people pushing each other to move ahead. Missed this race of life!" Abdus stared at Abeedah giving her a confused look. He was unable to understand that how can anyone find peace in such chaos?

Abeedah, coming back to reality, "Now, the problem is we need to go to Ghatkopar, and I am left with only 50 bucks. We can't afford a cab, so the only option is the local train."

Abdus could feel his body getting numbed. He stood still. It was too much change in the world beyond his imagination. The people, noise, the constant buzz of horn reminded him of some war.

Suddenly his memory recapitulated a scene from the battlefield. The weight of his affair, the rattling sound of the sword under the burning sun, neighing of horses and roaring of elephants. An arrow hissed past his left ear. The screeching sound of chariot wheels on the dry land, bloodbath and which flowed through the stream. The scream of soldiers.

The whole ground covered with the banners of red and gold and then, he saw his father, beheaded body falling on the ground, arrows bulging from his chest in the blood which made his eyes lifeless. A scream left him, and all he could see was a flag with an image of half human and half monkey waving proudly in the breeze.

Abeedah shouted, pulling him back from his flashback, "Abdus! Abdus! You are standing in the middle of the road, move! We need to go." Abeedah freaked out as Abdus's eyes turned red, and anger on his face. Tears were filled in his eyes. Abeedah got scared by his look. All this while traffic got stuck, and the crowd started shouting, "Move you weirdo, move!"

"Are you okay?" Abeedah asked hesitating.

Abdus tried to calm himself. He closed his eyes to control his emotions and nodded positively. They took a local train and got into a general compartment. Because of Abdus's weird dress and an unusual look, people started staring at him. It was for the first time Abdus was under such kind of situation. Gradually, he began feeling vulnerable. He could sense difficulty in breathing. It was an anxiety attack.

Abeedah got tensed and asked, "What is happening? Take a deep breath. Are you okay?"

Abeedah tried to console him by holding his hand. Abdus looked at a baby who was on her mother's arm. He was smiling and gazing at Abdus. He tried to focus on her innocent face started taking deep breaths. He was trying to distract himself to dodge his anxiety attack. After few minutes, he was back to his usual condition. "Children are wonders!" He thought.

Announcement "Next station Kurla."

People started pushing each other to get down early.

Abdus asked her, "Why are they in such a rush?"

Abeedah answered him, "Well, The train stops at every station for few seconds. It is not safe to stand near the door, but you are too tall to fit inside. The hangers will hit your head!"

In this rush of getting to the door, a man pushed the lady who was holding that baby. She was about to fell when Abdus managed to save her.

"Thank you mister.", the lady thanked Abdus and started patting her baby.

Abeedah, "Is she okay sister?" pointing at her baby.

Lady replied with a smile, "Yes she is fine."

Abeedah said with disappointment, "Why are these people so insensitive? Why can't they see that they were hurting an innocent life?"

Hearing her thoughts, Abdus had a vision from his past. An arrow was moving in speed and burning in fire. The temperature around raising like a volcano during an eruption and reaching towards a beautiful young pregnant woman in royal clothes and jewellery. Her hands were wrapping her womb, protecting her unborn child from the wrath of that powerfully chanted arrow. The whole room echoed with the clinking sound of bangles and scream of an agonising mother.

Announcement distracted Abdus from his thoughts "Next station Ghatkopar." Abeedah told him, "We are up next!"

Abeedah's voice brought him back to the reality. They got down and started walking towards Abeedah's home. Throughout their way, they were unable to ignore the stare of the people. She could sense the fear in their eyes because of Abdus's physical built. It was the night when they reached Abeedah's apartment.

For Abdus, everything was new and unseen. Abeedah went inside the lift of her building, but Abdus felt weird to get inside a five by five rectangular box whose gate was being opened and closed by an unknown force. There were already four men and two women inside the lift who were giving him a frowning look. The elevator was waiting for Abdus to get into it.

Abeedah pulled his hand, "Abdus get inside. We need to go to the 6th floor." Abdus sighed and nodded. He stood straight, but because of his surface area, he occupied the majority of the space. This made others pushed towards the wall unwillingly. As the elevators ascended, Abdus felt a slight pull in his stomach. Once the elevator stopped Abeedah pulled him again, "This is my floor." She signalled him to get out of the lift. She could see Mr. Tawde releasing his breath as Abdus stepped out of the elevator. Abeedah gave him an apologising smile. They came in front of a door. She took out a small bronze key which was behind a lamp stand. All this while Abdus was silent. But his silence could not hide his nervousness of being around the people.

Abdus was trying to adjust to this new environment. For days, he couldn't step out of the door. Abeedah was amazed to see all his scars vanishing so quickly except for the one on his forehead.

The hardest part of coming back was to explain everyone around about Shad, Ragini, and Siddhant, especially to their parents. Shad's parents always treated her like their daughter. After so many months when she met Shad's parents, they hugged her tightly and cried for hours. They told her how they were searching for them for months and Police were doing search and rescue missions but couldn't find them, They found Shad and Ragini's body and flew them back to Mumbai for burial. How they thought that she and Siddhant had died too. She was too heartbroken to realise that she couldn't even attend the funerals of her beloved friend and Fiancé. Abeedah's survival somewhere crushed her with an overwhelming guilt.

All this while, she had focused on her survival. She couldn't have the time to mourn the death of her loved ones. But now, while meeting their families, grief consumed her immensely. She promised Shad's parents to always be in their lives and not become a stranger now that Shad was dead.

When she came back to home, she saw Abdus who was sitting on the floor, trying to figure out how TV worked. A fresh wave of tears aroused her pain. She collapsed on the floor, and while crying, her body was shivering. She felt choked and had a feeling that she may not survive anymore when she heard a voice telling her to breathe. Abdus was stooping in front of her. He was helping her to calm down. Abdus, in a consoling tone, "Everything will be fine gradually. It was not your fault." She knew it. Instead of those words, it was his heavy voice that was rescuing her.

She could breathe again and started feeling a weird kind of peace. After all these months, she kept wondering if she could ever forget Shad. Now she knew that Shad would always remain in her life, not physically but in her memories. This pain used to etch her heart but sadly this was the final goodbye to her loved ones.

She was back to her daily life. Going back to the hospital was the only option that kept her away from the pain though it was hard. The doctors had presumed that she was dead and they had mourned her. It was a surprise when she went back and one of her colleague actually screamed thinking that she was a ghost. It was hilarious but sad at the same time. Then they crowded her asking about her and how she survived. She answered them patiently leaving a lot of parts, mostly about Abdus. While she was happy to be back at her job, she was still a little restless.

Abdus used to meditate most of the times. He couldn't step out of the door till yet. Whenever Abeedah was back from the hospital, she always found him enjoying the sunset and listen to the chirping of the birds from the window. It was his favourite pass time. He used to spend hours enjoying it.

Abeedah always admired Abdus for his lifestyle. He still kept himself busy with meditation and yoga. Every morning she used to make coffee for him. Abdus loved coffee. One fine evening when she came back from work, Abdus was not in his usual place. She started frantically looking for him and found him in the kitchen.

Abeedah asked, "What are you doing in the kitchen?"

He replied over his shoulder, "Making coffee."

It was an amusing view for Abeedah to find him in the kitchen. The way he measured coffee and sugar with little spoons reminded her the story of Gulliver's Travels. Abeedah could sense his dedication level through his actions.

"I am a little late today, but if you had waited for me, I would have made it for you…" she suggested.

"This is not for me. This one is for you." Abdus said with full concentration on his coffee making.

Abeedah smiled "Wow. Someone is lucky today! But when did you learn to make coffee?"

"I watch you every morning." He replied with intensity.

They sat together on the sofa, watching the sunset, drinking coffee. This was bliss.

She took a sip of her coffee. "This is good. I must say you are a fast learner!"

He said amused, "You don't know many things about me."

The next day, Abeedah decided to take Abdus out, for shopping. She could see how he had isolated himself from the outer world. She did not like Abdus wearing those weird clothes all the time, but he seemed content with it. She had brought him a few pair of shirts, kurta and pants along with some footwear which were hard to find as he wore XXL in everything, but they weren't gong to cut out if he wanted to live in the world and live somewhat normally. She took him to the nearest mall. Abdus was not used to this kind of civilisation, and again he felt uncomfortable. He tried to maintain his calm and followed Abeedah's advice in everything.

Abeedah took him to the men's clothing section which was on the second floor. For her escalator was a usual thing but for Abdus it was something strange which was not at all easy to climb, when it was in constant movement. Abeedah reached the second floor and looked around for Abdus, who was still standing on the first floor looking at people and how they manage to climb on the moving staircase.

Abeedah who herself was like a child at heart, felt like she was babysitting a handsome, innocent but a grown up child. She came down as fast as she could without making Abdus notice that she was gone, stood by his side, held his hand and helped him with the escalator.

They entered a shop and looked at him, his eyes wide taking in all the things in the store. They selected few T-shirts, shirts and pants along with some sweatpants in his size. Abdus enjoyed trying number of shirts and Abeedah enjoyed looking at his shyness turning to excitement. He looked handsome in everything he tried and women around him kept checking him out, making Abeedah jealous which was strange as she never felt jealous. She was never jealous when she was with Shad, who was her Fiancé. Ignoring her wayward thoughts, she took Abdus to footwear section for him to buy some shoes. After getting some necessary toiletries and essentials for Abdus, they went to checkout corner to pay for all they had bought, which were a lot.

While heading towards the exit door of the showroom, Abdus eyes stuck on a mannequin wearing a classy black suit. Abeedah saw him gazing at the suit and she also wondered how he would look in that suit, keeping in mind his enormous stature. She prodded Abdus to try it on and after some pleading he relented. She asked the store helper to help Abdus with that suit. While he was in the trial room, Abeedah was waiting outside searching for the right pair of shoes for him.

After few minutes, she heard Abdus calling her name.

She turned back and froze as her heart skipped a beat looking at him. She couldn't believe her eyes. A man living in those caves, whose face once terrified her, now looks so handsome, she had trouble keeping her eyes off his face. In that black suit, he was the most stunning man she had ever seen. She couldn't resist herself drowning in those perfect dark brown eyes.

"So, how do I look?" he asked, self conscious when he saw that Abeedah was gaping at him without saying a word.

Shaking herself back from her awestruck, she replied, "Handsome! We are definitely getting this one."

Abeedah asked him to wait outside while she went to pay the bill. Abdus couldn't ignore the starring eyes of the ladies walking inside the mall. He got nervous and held his head down to ditch any eye contact. He was unaware of the fact that they were perusing him in curiosity and not critically. Then he felt a soft touch of a hand on his wrist, Abeedah's touch gave him a confidence to walk tall in the cold ignoring all the staring eyes.

Abeedah took him for dinner in a Chinese restaurant after their shopping. Again, everyone in the diner admired him for the way he looks. It was easy to see jealousy in the eyes of men and lust in women around them, but he never noticed it. He was least interested in all the available attention. Abeedah was having all his undivided attention. And she realised that she liked it. Waiter brought them the menu. Surprisingly, he could read and pronounce every dish accurately even the specials, which was written in Mandarin. The only difference was that he was not aware what the dishes actually were.

Abeedah asked curiously, "Whoa! You know how to read Mandarin?"

He replied casually "I know a lot of languages!"

"But how?"

"I traveled a lot."

"Without passport?"

"Passport?"

"Oh! It is kind of a travel permit to travel other countries."

He chuckled at her innocence and ignored her question. She hated when he didn't answer her which he did a lot but he never wanted to make him feel uncomfortable with her questions, so she did not repeat it. Still, it used to hit her mind regarding what Abdus would have been hiding which restricts him so uncomfortable to answer.

While Abeedah was busy ordering their dinner, Abdus was observing a couple sitting next to their table. The way they were interacting, attracted his attention. They seemed lost in their world. The lady was wearing a bright green satin long dress with her hair loosely tied in a loose braid.

His man was laughing as he tucked loose strand of her hair behind her ear. This made the lady blush all. Then he looked at Abeedah whose hair always covered with hijab. He started noticing that couple again. The couple after finishing off their dinner and the man paid the bill. He stood up first and then pulled her lady's chair and took her hand and walked away.

Abdus, who was not with a woman for so long, keenly observed the couple's actions. He realised this fact that women these days want themselves treated like a queen. Gone are those days where the title of the queen was enough and felt honoured by sharing a standard seat with their king. He was lost in thoughts when their food was placed in front of them.

After dinner, Abeedah paid the bill. Abdus felt humiliated as he had no money to treat her properly. He tried to imitate from the actions of that couple. He pulled Abeedah's chair, and she was impressed by his sudden chivalry of Abdus.

As they stepped outside, she pointed to a park at a distance, its benches where men and women of all ages, sat and spent quality time with their friend or partner. Some of them were enjoying their solitude. It was a lonely park in solitary with no building or houses around it nearby.

"That is my fortress of solitude!" Abdus gave her a confused look.

Abeedah explained further, "Whenever I am sad or confused, I go there and sit for hours."

Abdus smiled at her. He didn't know how to react to such kind of conversation with a woman. He never considered women in his life with so much of interest. While she was calling a cab, he suggested walking their way back to home.

After the not so romantic dinner but with a little desire inside they left for home. On their way back, they saw a drunken man brutally beating her wife. He was dragging her on the floor byre hair.

Abeedah ran towards the lady and yelled at the man.

"What the hell are you doing?"

"She is my wife. I can do whatever I want with her."

"Back off! She's your wife, not your property."

Abeedah tried togged the man off the woman but, he pushed Abeedah with such force that she fell down hitting her shoulder. This angered Abdus. He closed his fist, and the veins on his hand bulged out. He pulled the man by his arm and threw him at a distance like trash. Abeedah couldn't believe her eyes. She immediately ran to stop him. She tried to push Abdus, but her hands were not enough to succeed her attempt. He was so blind in his uncontrollable rage that he pushed her aside. She landed on her hands. Her hands were scratched badly, pain shot through her hands, and her yelp caught Abdus's attention. He saw her lying on the ground holding her left hand. His rage transformed itself into guilt. She was injured because of him. Her tears ripped his heart apart.

He was immediately by her side and asked her softly."I am sorry. I am so sorry, Are you okay?"

She just nodded. Fear was evident in her eyes. She scared enough to not let him touch her bleeding hands.

The wife thanked him, still shocked and ran to check her husband who was now unconscious. They called a cab and went back to their home. Abeedah looked out through the window the whole time in the cab. She did not even give him a slight glance, and this left Abdus with a feeling of being worse than the dirt.

The silence in the taxi took him back to the place where he was a witness of a woman's humiliation who had a warrior spirit. A woman, epitome of beauty. Her beautiful long hair clutched by some evil hands of a prince who dragged her into the court. She had an unstoppable fire in her eyes while questioning the court that what gave her husband the right to bet her in a gamble.

The humiliation of a woman, witnessed by strongest of men, couldn't do anything but watched her getting disrobed and witnessed a miracle. How, even though she had been humiliated by her husband, she used her wishes in saving her husbands and sons. Worse, Abdus thought her as dirty and deserving of what was happening to her. He felt utterly ashamed today for his thoughts. Now he understood how a war started as a retaliation of her humiliation by staring at Abeedah who was watching the outside scene from the cab.

Her face made him believe that he would go to any war for her. Her strong personality, her passion, her humility, her beauty was beyond the worth of praising. The spark of her eyes reminded him of that humiliated woman, Draupadi.

As they reached home, she put the bags away, then pulled out a box, sat on the sofa and started cleaning her wounds. Abdus was unable to ignore her pain which came on her face as the wounds started to sting. She was still silent. Abdus went up to her. He held her hand, in spite of her resistance, he started cleaning the blood.

He said in a soft voice,"I don't have any intention of hurting you. At that time, I was unable to control myself when I saw that man hurting and disrespecting you. In my life, I have done wrongful deeds for which I am not proud. I always thought of a woman as a thing, whose sole purpose is to please her man and to give birth to their heir.

In spite of having all the attributes of a human, I regret being one. I did not try to understand a woman. I never thought they are worthy enough of giving importance. But with you? It's different. Whenever I see you, I feel how wrong I was. I am a dishonour of being a man. I have lost all my hopes of living my life again. I am breathing just to suffer. With you, I want to live. I want to know you better. I want to know what makes you laugh, what makes you sad, everything…"

After listening to him, Abeedah's fearful expression turned into a charming smile.

Abeedah asked softly and curiously "Are you married?"

"No!"

"So whom are you talking about?" She asked.

"I wish I could tell you one day." He replied.

After their conversation, Abeedah was much more determined to learn the truth.

After covering her wounds with bandages, he put on some music. He had eclectic taste in music but had special love for Alternate Rock. Whenever he used to listen to country Rock, he used to feel like a free bird for a short period. He had a sheer sharp memory that he used to remember the lyrics word by word just by listening to a song for once. Abeedah very often found him humming this tune.

Slowly Abdus tried to come out of his comfort zone. He started communicating with the neighbours, and soon they in the building. Mrs. Harshvardhan, their nearest neighbour and a kind widow, considered him as his brother. She always used to cook a different kind of dishes for him to taste. It was quite evident from his physic that Abdus was a food lover.

One fine morning, Mrs. Harshvardhan rang Abeedah's doorbell. Abdus somewhat knew that it should be Mrs. Harshvardhan as, during this time of the day, she used to surprise him with her delicious food. He opened the door in excitement. It was her but not with food. Abdus found her seven-year-old son peeking from her back.

Mrs. Harshvardhan smiled at him, "Good morning Abdus. Sorry I couldn't surprise you this time with my food. I came here to seek a major help…"

Abdus instantly replied, "Sure, how may I help you?"

"My mother is very sick, and she is hospitalised. I have to go to see her. Can I leave Ryan with you? His exams are starting from tomorrow. Can you please take care of him till I return?"

Abdus looked at the child, "I would love to help you Mrs. Harshvardhan, but I am not sure if I am good at dealing with children..."

Mrs. Harshvardhan in an assuring tone, "Oh! Don't worry about that. Ryan will not irritate you."

She hugged Ryan. "Be a good boy and study. Ask uncle Abdus if you need anything. Okay?"

Ryan was scared of Abdus. He politely nodded to his mother's question obediently.

Abdus and Ryan bid goodbye to her and made Ryan sit on the dining table.

"So what exam do you have tomorrow?" Abdus asked Ryan.

"Science" Ryan replied timidly.

"Okay! You study. I am sitting there." He said pointing towards the couch.

After few hours he discovered that Ryan was so afraid of him that neither did he speak a single word throughout nor he asked for going to the loo.

Abdus asked Ryan, "Do you want to play something?"

"Okay," he replied with a curious look.

He searched the whole flat to find a game to play, but the only thing he found was a chess board. He picked up a notepad and a pencil and called Ryan to sit on the couch beside him.

"Now tell me who is your favourite superhero is?" Abdus asked.

"Umm… Ironman!" Ryan replied with excitement.

"And most favourite villain?"

"Joker."

Abdus nodded and drew a multi-tier structure of seven rounds that looked like a disc. He placed the black knight at the central point of the disc and set the white knight outside the structure.

"The black knight is Joker, and white knight is Ironman. Now, each tier of the disc is made up of soldiers who are protecting Joker, and the disc is continuously rotating like a wheel to keep your Ironman in a state of wondering how to break each tier, how to get to the Joker. The soldiers in the inner layer are stronger than the soldiers standing on the outer layer. In every tier, there is one spot with no soldier, but it is a trap! Now tell me how you will break all the tiers and kill the joker?" Abdus explained patiently.

"I will kill the soldier in front of Ironman and sneak into the second tier, and in the same manner my Ironman will pass through all the tiers to kill Joker," Ryan explained his strategy after giving deep thought to it.

"No, you can't do that. Observe that the soldiers are always in motion. If you kill the soldier in front of Ironman, the soldier on his left will take the assassinated soldier's place. They will fill the gap again, and your Ironman is blocked!" Abdus said. Ryan thought of different options and theories but gave up in the end.

He said disappointed, "There is no way he can kill the Joker. It is impossible!" He sighed loudly and lied down in the couch, which made Abdus laugh.

"Well, don't be so dramatic. Here, I'll tell you how. See, if you shoot the soldiers standing on left and right of your Ironman quickly, this will force them into creating a movement of to cover up the gaps. For a concise period, the gap will stay vacant in front of you from where you can sneak into the tiers. Don't forget to take your strong army with you otherwise; your Ironman will get trapped inside!" Abdus explained. Ryan gave him a confused look. He laughed at his expression.

"Lesson of the story is that nothing is impossible!" Abdus chuckled softly.

"Who taught you this game?" Ryan asked curiously.

"My father. He invented it," he replied with pride.

"Really?? What he used to call this game?"

"He used to call it "The Chakravyuha."

They hear a knock at the door; it was Abeedah.

Abeedah came inside and said, "Ryan, your mom is here."

Ryan said to Abdus cheerfully, "Bye uncle! Oh, I forgot! Can you take me to the fair? I have asked mom so many times, but she is always busy." He made an innocent face.

"Aahh..." Abdus in a vague tone.

Ryan insisted, "Please uncle! Please!"

Abdus smiled and agreed " Okay, if your mom agrees, I will then." Ryan let out a cheer and went to his mom to ask who agreed. They both thanked Abdus and went to their home.

Abeedah was amazed to this side of him, "Well, it seems you are a kid charmer now, huh?"

"He is a good boy." Abdus blushed and went to make coffee.

Chapter Nine

Are you like Arjun?

The next day, Ryan was all excited and dressed up for the fair. Abdus was very punctual with time. Abeedah handed some money to Abdus. He gave her a clueless look. "Take this. You will need it." She smiled.

The fair was all illuminated by light everywhere. Under the blanket of darkness, the place appeared like a firefly. Ryan was super excited, and so was Abdus. It was his and Abdus's first outing in this new world. They halted at every stall of food and game. Abdus being a food lover tasted every fast food of the fair. While exploring, Abdus' eyes caught the attention of an archery stall named "Are you like Arjun?" This statement provoked him.

He picked up the bow and shot all the target at level one in a quick sequence. The most eye-catching moment was a shot of three arrows all together which flew at a bullet speed. It was almost invisible for the people to determine the arrow. This caught the attention of the crowd, and everyone started applauding him especially a well-suited gentleman who was the manager of that fair.

He approached Abdus and said, "Hello, my name is Rajat Singh. I saw your performance, and it was amazing."

Abdus smiled and said, "Thank you Rajat, My name is Abdus Samad."

"I was wondering if you could teach my son this wonderful talent you have. Honestly, I have never seen anyone as skilled as you!"

"Well, I am not sure—"

"I will pay you well! My son is very much interested in archery, and I don't think I can find anyone better than you."

Right from the beginning of his journey till now, Abdus had realised a fact that to survive in this world, money is significant. He thought that it is an excellent opportunity to earn and without thinking twice, he accepted the offer.

"It will be my pleasure to teach your son."

Rajat gave him his visiting card and asked him to start his coaching from the next day itself.

Excitedly and feeling proud enough, Abdus and Ryan returned home. Hiding his excitement, he did not say anything to Abeedah. The next day, he woke up and before she could get up, he left for his first coaching class.

Abdus unknowingly made a sweet gesture. He left a note for Abeedah which said, "Don't worry. I am going somewhere…will be back soon." After reading this post it, she giggled at his childishness. She was worried and thought of all the possible places where he could go. Abeedah was well aware of his innocence and the cruelty of this world.

Abdus had to ask a lot of people for directions and how trains worked but he finally reached his destination. Abdus reached Rajat's house where Rajat introduced him to his son, Manik. He was thirteen years old, skinny and bald. He had a lethargic appearance reflecting that he was exhausted.

"This is Manik, my son. Manik, this is Mr. Abdus, your archery teacher from today." Rajat smiled.

"Hello, sir." Manik greeted warmly to Abdus.

"Manik, go to your practice room. Mr. Abdus will be there in few minutes."

After Manik left, Rajat informed Abdus about Manik's condition.

"I love my son more than anything in this world, but God is forever testing my perseverance. I lost my wife while she was giving birth to Manik and he was a stillborn baby. I think God pitied on my condition and somehow he started breathing. Still, in this world, everything comes with a price. He granted him his breath but, Manik is suffering from Insomnia. But it is even worse with him. He sleeps for minutes, an hour at most which makes him lethargic and weak. It is now clearly visible on his skin. I am doing all I can to treat him but….."

He gave Abdus sardonic smile and continued, "When I saw you yesterday, I thought this might make Manik happy. I have contacted many trainers, but they all refused because of his situation. They communicated it politely that they don't want to waste their time. I can understand if you too don't want to coach him."

"I had a friend whom no one considered worthy enough of being an archer. Everyone rejected him from their training even my father, but he never gave up. He even lied to achieve his goal, and he turned out to be one of the finest archers, they knew! Rajat, my choice of selecting students, is above someone's abilities or disabilities, caste or religion. His passion to learn is what I seek for…" Abdus replied, referring to great Karna.

Rajat's heart filled with happiness. He now had a ray of hope for his son. With teary eyes, he shook his hand with Abdus and gave him a bundle of notes as his first salary.

Abdus felt blessed. The next thought was now he can also treat Abeedah in the same way in that guy was entertaining his lady in the Chinese restaurant. He went into the training room and saw Manik standing all prepared. He was holding an unusual bow with multi-threaded and iron fitting.

"So why want to become an archer?" Abdus asked to break the ice between them.

"I want to be like my father."

"But your father is not an archer. Is he?"

Manik gave him a indifferent smile but did not answer him.

Abdus started his training telling him about positions and where to keep hands and science behind archery.

After completing his first session, he was happy and satisfied. Manik was a quick learner and excellent student. Now, with his first class over, he wanted to surprise Abeedah. While passing through a local market, he stopped at a showroom. He went inside and precisely explained the dress he wanted to gift her. It was the same emerald satin gown which the lady in the restaurant was wearing.

The showroom had the same dress but in red and white. Without wasting much of his time, he picked up the red one. He also stopped at the bakery shop and got packed all the delicious items he could find there and reach home. Abdus started having strange feelings for Abeedah, and he practiced a lot as to how he would romantically disclose the surprise. There was a low flutter in his stomach whenever he thought about her of saw her.

It was quite difficult for him because he was neither much experienced with women's emotion nor with romantic gestures. In the evening, he placed all the cakes and sweets he bought from the bakery shop on the table and waited for her.

He heard the clinking of the keys behind the door. Before Abeedah could unlock the door, Abdus opened it for her. She finally felt relieved after seeing him and stared at him suspiciously, "Where have been the whole—"

She was surprised looking at the display all over the table. A gift box lying on the couch caught her attention. She smiled and teased, "Mr. Abdus what are you up to?"

He handed her the gift box. Surprised Abeedah asked him, "But from where? I mean how you managed to…"

He interrupted her in the middle and said: "Try this, and I will tell you everything."

In a curious and shocked state of mind, she went to her room and unwrapped the gift. Meanwhile, Abdus couldn't control his urge for sweets and started eating pastries. By the time she was all dressed and came out, only two pieces of the cakes were left.

She looked gorgeous in that red gown. His heart skipped a beat, and he felt his knees go weak. He started feeling butterflies flutter inside his stomach, and his throat felt dry. He even forgot to blink his eyes. He felt grave difficulty in uttering a single word, but he knew he had to say something to chase her attention. It was for the first time he saw her in loose hair.

He said shyly, "You look beautiful."

She smiled and thanked him. While they ate the remaining pastries, Abdus told her about his new job, his student and how was his first day. Abeedah was extremely happy and excited as she asked, "So how is Manik?"

"Intelligent. His appearance covers his power of understanding. He tends to second guess everything he is presented with. He is quite logical and sincere. I am sure he has a great future ahead, no matter how long he lives." Abdus replied.

Throughout his explanation, there was never a moment where his eyes left her face. Abeedah sensing his nervousness suggested playing music and she took the initiative. She started music player and the notes of "Can't help falling in love with you" filled the air. She had softness in her eyes as she wanted to convey that this was what she wanted to say to Abdus. Abdus took her and started swaying as he has seen in movies and they danced, they laughed and got carried away into their universe.

Abdus touched a stray lock of hair which made his way on her face falling on her face and tucked it behind her ear. They were close and getting closer without realizing and their lips were tipping towards each other. Finally, Abdus couldn't control himself, and he kissed her. Abeedah saw it all coming, and she was living that moment. She gently moved her hands from his bicep to his jaw framing his face. He grabbed her by her lower waist with his right hand and buried the left one in her hair.

It was electric and a connection that they did not want to end. It was soft and fierce at the same time. Finally they both came up for hair and touched their forehead together. Abdus chuckled softly, "I did not plan this!"

"Neither did I" She whispered. She was too shy to say anything more. She pressed her head on his chest and took a moment to lower her heart beat. With a blush on her face "Amm… Well for a caveman, you are an excellent kisser!"

"In my days, I have been with a lot of women" He replied humorously.

"I don't mind." She replied confidently touching his face.

"I mean a lot of women" he tried to tease her.

She punched him lightly in his chest saying, "Oh! Just shut up." It was a new found romantic moment for both of them, and they got lost in each other while kissing again and again. It was an unexpected attraction which was quite subtle deep down in their heart. Abeedah, with a pounding heart, confessed her feelings. "I love you, Abdus."

Hearing those words, Abdus completely forgot about his past and future. He was stuck in that one moment. He never wanted to hurt Abeedah because she was unaware of who he was. He confessed, "I love you so much more than I could ever imagine but you don't know my past, my reality."

She lifted her right eyebrow and asked: "So are you going to reveal your past now?"

"Even if I tell you, you won't understand. I am cursed to suffer. I bring demolition to everything I touch." He replied in a sad tone.

"You don't know my past either. I am an orphan. I never saw my mother. I don't even remember my father's face. He handed me to his friend and eloped. I stayed with his friend's family. He never discriminated me with his children. Encouraged me to study medicine and become a doctor. A few years back, I lost him in flood. After his death and I was thrown out of his house as I was not legally authorized to live there. The worst which I thought for you was an alien. Even you are, my feelings will not change. I know you did some awful things in your past but now you are a different person, and I believe in this person standing in front of me." she said by patting his chest.

"If things are meant to go wrong, it will go. Who knows what lies in future, but right now? It's us. You and I, it feels complete, it feels right. We both have suffered a lot, and I think we both are cursed to suffer. So why don't we begin our journey of suffering together? I have never felt this contented and safe."

Abdus loved her beyond his words, beyond what he thought he was capable of.

After listening to her words, he fell under her spell. He found her explanation to be quite sensible. It was after meeting her, his wounds started healing. His old heart was beating like a teenager. He grabbed and kissed her again. She laid her on the couch, but she pushed him back and asked, "When you said you have been with a lot of women, who were they?"

Abdus chuckled and said "I don't know. I don't even know their names."

"You paid them?" she asked hesitantly

"Yes, most of them. Others came willingly."

"What!"

"Come on, have you looked at me? I was a royal." he spilled in a flow.

She raised her eyebrows, "Royalty?"

"I mean I did some royal work, and it was a long time ago, it was altogether a different era. I am not that person now. You can trust me." he assured her by holding her hand.

She nodded with a smile. "I do trust you."

They made love that night. It was an unforgettable night for both of them. With each shed of clothe, they also shed their insecurity, uncertainty and pain. It was a union of two hearts and bodies who have found their safe haven in each other. It was for the first time for Abdus he united with a woman's soul, not the body, and it was for the first time for Abeedah who looked at Abdus as his love and not as a compatible partner. Under the covering of darkness and moonlight, they gifted their respect to each other.

Chapter Ten

The truth

Abeedah woke up late the next morning. She had a peaceful night in the arms of Abdus. After a long time, she was at peace. She saw him wearing a crisp white shirt and denim. His wet hair, perfectly combed and his smile completed his look. Whether it was the suit or denim, it appeared as if all it was made for his toned body and chiseled looks.

"You look delicious! I must say that although, being a caveman, you have a good taste in clothes!" she teased him while running her fingers through her messy hair

"I made you morning coffee." He smiled and gave her the mug. She thanked him and sighed at its taste. His love had made her a little girl again who has loved to cherish little moments of joy even at terrible times. He kissed her forehead and bid her goodbye for the day. Abdus walked towards the door, and Abeedah called him,

"Wait! I have a surprise for you. But I completely forgot when I saw—"

While talking, she went to her room, but Abdus couldn't focus on her talk. He was still reliving those moments from the last night. She came back with two boxes in her hand.

"Here, this one is for you and one is for me." It was a cell phone.

"What is this? I don't need a compass! Don't worry; I won't get lost. You will always find me near you as the night will fall." He said in an assuring tone.

Abeedah chuckled at his innocence. "This is not a compass! It's a gadget which can do a lot of things apart from the compass. It has internet where you can search for anything and any subject you want to know. You will learn it once you use. This will help us to stay connected whenever we want to. You can talk to me anytime by using it. I have already saved my number in your set."

"Oh! I thought it's a compass because I often find people staring down at it all the time." He took his set, listened to Abeedah as she told him how to call her. Abdus kissed her and left for the day.

Abeedah was not a deeply religious person. Still, she thought of seeking the blessings of Allah for her newly deep-rooted relationship given they both did not have the presence of an elderly in their lives. So she decided to pick Abdus up to go to mosque. When he asked where they were going, but she refused to answer telling him it was a surprise. On their way, she took Abdus's hand. Unaware of the place, when Abdus got a hint of where he was going, his steps took a halt on climbing the ladders of the Mosque.

"Abdus? What happened? Let's go inside." Abeedah tried to move ahead, but Abdus hand was firm enough not even to move an inch.

"I am not an atheist. I just don't believe he—," he stopped for a while, gave a blank stare and hesitantly said, "They can help me…"

"I believe that people often come here just to thank them and not just to seek his or their help. Today, I am here just to thank Allah for bringing you into my life." She explained.

"You go. I will wait for you here, till you return." his tone was now adamant.

Abeedah went inside, and Abdus went to the nearby fruit market to get some fruits. His senses were stronger than that of an ordinary man as he started smelling every fruit which was in the stall. Besides him, there was an old lady who was also purchasing some fruits. She made her payment and said her farewells to the vendor by saying "Jai Shri Krishna!"

Abdus immediately froze upon hearing the words and couldn't believe his ears. It had been a really long time that he has heard his name. His nerves got stunned for a while on hearing such words. His eyes grew wide open and immediately asked that old lady, "What did you just say?"

"Jai Shri Krishna. We greet people by saying this. It means long live lord Krishna." She smiled.

Abdus's face turned red in anger. He quietly followed that old lady. She stopped at a temple. He went inside the temple, and the view enraged her rage to the extreme. Abdus saw that the people were worshiping the statue of Krishna. He couldn't believe that how so many people were still glorifying a man who is a trickster in his eyes.

Meanwhile, Abeedah came outside the mosque and looked around for Abdus. She tried calling him, but the call went unanswerable. She got frightened and started looking for him in the area. Soon, she saw him standing on the stairs of a temple. By the time Abeedah could have called him, he shouted "Why are you worshipping him? He is not a god! He was just a good wizard and a trickster. He is not even worthy of anyone's worship!" His eyes turned solid red as Lava. Those were not of sadness but anger.

A man stood up to retaliate, "How can you say that? He is our faith. He is our savior!"

Abeedah sensed a severe danger approaching Abdus. She immediately ran towards him and asked him to move on, but Abdus's anger overpowered him and even denied to notice her presence. Abdus had a mockery laugh and continued, "What savior? He didn't save anyone. He was a big time cheater. A conniving demon that always ensured that things happen as per his benefit."

Meanwhile, a crowd gathered because of such chaos. A man standing next to him shouted in anger. "How dare you speak in this way of our God? Do not speak ill of his name otherwise you will face a dreadful outcome!"

Enraged by the people's blind belief, he lifted a statue of a lion statue which was placed for decoration next to him. People around him got frightened, and no sooner they tried to stop him, Abdus threw the figure at the idol of Krishna. The statue broke into pieces just like a building collapses in an earthquake within few seconds.

For a minute, everything around paused. People couldn't believe their eyes. Some were in profound shock, and some got scared because of the extraordinary power of Abdus. Abeedah felt as if the air was knocked out of her lungs, and she cried, "Yah Allah!" Her words led to a rise in sudden outburst in the crowd. Their God was attacked by a Muslim.

Within few minutes, Abeedah noticed a colossal crowd running towards them in anger. Abdus had a strange fear of crowds. His brain stopped for a second, and he was unable to register what kind of danger was approaching him. He failed to understand that what crime he has committed which has ignited a sense of hatred amongst the people towards him.

Abeedah grabbed his hand, and they both ran towards the main road. The crowd was fiercely running after them for the revenge. While running, Abeedah heard a voice from the back. "Catch that giant! He is a Muslim. It's their conspiracy to harm us again! This time, we are not going to leave them!"

Abeedah somehow managed to hop into the first available cab. "Driver, please take us out of this area," Abeedah shouted in fear. "But where do you want to go?" asked the cab driver. "I will tell you everything but first take us out of this area safely and quickly!!"

She was panting while talking to the driver and all this while Abdus was trying hard to figure out the situation and chaos. She looked back from the glass and saw some of the people were still searching them. She immediately asked Abdus to stoop down and hide so that they won't get caught. All this while, the cab was marking its way out of the area.

Abeedah peeked outside and founded herself in a safer area. She immediately turned around Abdus and shouted "What is the matter with you? Are you insane? Do you know what you have done and what are its repercussions? Once you are caught, they will simply kill you! Have you lost—?"

"I am NOT sorry for what I did and said there!" He interrupted her in anger.

"But, why? I know that you don't believe in God, but it doesn't mean you will disrespect other's beliefs. It attacks people's emotions. That is not justified!" He remained quiet. Abeedah got really scared and worried about the safety of Abdus. They came back home by evening. Abeedah didn't say a word all night and Abdus had no idea what to say to her. Silence was not at all golden and it was stretched all through the night.

The next morning, there was still radio silence between them. After making their coffee, Abdus went to sit in the balcony while Abeedah sat on sofa and randomly switched on the TV. She found that the yesterday's incident was all over the news channels. Fear struck her heart. She had never thought in her wildest dreams that such would be the outcome of Abdus's action.

"Yes. You heard it right. Different parts of the nation are under the situation of the riot. The fire of riot ignited from an area of Mumbai where a mysterious man had been charged with harming the idol of Lord Krishna in a temple. The witness of the situation is claiming that the giant belonged to the Muslim community.

Immediately after the incident, people from the Hindu community had portrayed their anger by burning the houses of Muslim families. To counterpart, Muslims had also retaliated to their actions in the same manner. Now the incident had turned into a national riot. Communal fights have been noticed in various parts of the states. Till far 106 people have lost their lives and around 200 people are injured. Many children and women are lost, and we guess our police is helpless to take charge of this situation.

Nobody thought that a small fight of a small area would lead to such havoc. Famous areas of the cities have been found burning including temples, mosques, and churches. The Catholics had started blaming Protestants for being involved in such an inhuman activity. The news had affected the people from a different country as well.

People are protesting in their own way and questioning the silence of the government. A leader from the ruling party is claiming that it is all planned and several leaders of the opposition party are involved in it. Our citizens want to know that is this enough? Have communal rights won in their war with humanity? Tell us your views on our social media—", the rest was a blur to Abeedah as she stared at the TV. She could see the screen but couldn't hear anything as blood rushed to her ears.

After the headlines, the channel displayed a CCTV video from which one could recognise the silhouette of Abdus and Abeedah from the back but it wasn't clear enough to be a rock solid proof. She thanked Allah for that.

Abeedah quickly switched off her television. She never thought that Abdus's anger would take such a grave turn that it will harm so many people. She was numb. She could not understand what to do next.

"Thank God, they don't have Abdus's photo." She murmured.

It was not only the nation whose roots had been shaken but also the relationship of Abdus and Abeedah. They haven't shared much between them after the incident. Her silence was enough for Abdus to understand that he is the one responsible for the whole mess.

He could bear all kind of blame and anger, but when it directed from the side of Abeedah, it was unbearable for him. Abeedah's changed behaviour towards him ripped his heart. He could see the fear, a sense of disappointment and anger on her face. He immediately ran towards the door and ran outside the building. Abeedah ran after him because she was petrified for his safety. "Abdus. Stop! Where are you going? LISTEN TO ME…" But Abdus was running in his own rage.

He had no idea how long he ran or walked. He finally stopped and looked around and found himself at the same place which Abeedah had shown him as her place of solitude. It was deserted and couldn't see a soul for as long as his eyes could see clearly. This park was on the edge of a forest.

With heavy steps, he fell to his knees. There were unshed tears in his eyes. He kept thinking that this was his punishment that when he finally got some happiness in his life and it went away because he was stupid and couldn't control his anger. He should've known better than to believe that he would be happy again.

Abeedah came after him and saw him in this state from a distance. It was for the first time she was seeing him so defeated. She hid behind a tree as observed what he was going to do next. She could only hear some murmur of Abdus as if he was blaming himself for the lives which do not exist anymore. This brought tears to her eyes, but she found herself helpless.

The tears started falling from his eyes which he couldn't control anymore. As he cried, Abdus yelled in anger looking up at the sky. "Are you happy now? Can't you see people are killing each other in your name? What don't you stop them? What are you doing? Nothing! How very typical of you, Vasudev! That's what you know, and that's what you do. You trick them. You have tricked them to consider you as their God. They are a fool to think so highly you. You are no God! God is never partial. But you are!! You killed my father! You are just a cheater and a murderer."

He stood up and continued, "You are a coward Vasudev! You hear me? Coward! You are nothing but a cheater!"

He heard some footsteps against dry leaves on the ground. He turned around and saw Abeedah standing at a distance. Abdus realized that she had heard everything whatever he had said. It was beyond her knowledge to understand the meaning behind his words, anger, and tears.

She stood stunned. "Who are you?" She did not have that much of courage to stand near him. She maintained a calculated distance.

At this moment, Abdus realized that there was nothing left to hide and he was also afraid of losing her.

"Trust me you don't want to know." he replied in a sobbing voice.

"Who. Are. You?" she asked in a trembling voice.

She was shivering in fear. Her eyes had turned red because of crying. Abdus blamed himself for Abeedah's condition. Once again, he became the reason behind her tears. Agitated in anger, he cursed Krishna for making him stand on the verge of losing Abeedah, his life.

There was a sudden change in the atmosphere. The air grew heavy and the clouds were covering the sun making the sky gray. Winds were starting to blow making their clothes stick to their skin. But the storm outside had no match for the storm swirling inside Abdus.

"You want to know who I am? Really, are you sure? The moment I will disclose, you will run far away from me for eternity!" He shouted.

"Yes. I want to know who you are. I wanted to know since the day we have met! At least I have this much of right to learn about the person whom I love." She retaliated in anger.

This statement of hers made Abdus lost his control. He started behaving like a caged lion. With all his power and anger, he went towards the nearest tree and tore it apart from its roots. He appeared not less like a demon to her. The muscles of his face were all stretched because of the anger inside him. In no time, he threw away the tree in rage. Abeedah was petrified, and so was Abdus.

Abdus shouted in his own rage by spreading his arms on his sides, "You want to know the real me, right? Well, here I am, in all my glory and all my powers. I am not Abdus, I am Ashwatthama, the son of Dronacharya!"

The speed and intensity of wind grew harder and harder. Out of nowhere, loud winds of storm covered the sky, making it duller and grayer than before. Thunder was loud and booming. Abeedah could feel the pressure of wind and words of Abdus. She looked up at the sky, wondering if the sudden change in the atmosphere was because of Abdus. There was a strange aura of power around Abdus. She stood confused for a while and immediately turned her back from him and ran away, far away from Abdus, leaving him alone to face the storm.

Her life turned upside down, once again. With grave difficulty, she managed to come back to her flat. She was in the state of shock. She managed to escape the storm of nature, but she had no clue how to face this new storm which has entered her life for a further destruction. She sat at the corner of her room, folded her legs and cried her heart out. This was the tears of anxiety. These were the tears of unknown.

After some time, when she could feel a sense of control on herself, she realized what Abdus had told her. His real name. She immediately grabbed her laptop and typed his name 'Ashwatthama' on the search engine. With a click, her life changed forever, again!

Chapter eleven

The riot of religion

A few hours later, a defeated Abdus returned to the flat and found Abeedah sitting on the couch with her laptop, beside her. She was aimlessly staring the floor with a blank expression. Her eyes were red enough to say that they had cried a lot. He sat in front of her and for some time they both shared a heavy silence after the disastrous revelation. He saw her laptop opened in from of her on the table.

"So now you know?" he broke the silence by pointing towards the laptop. She nodded a yes.

"I know you have a lot of questions. Please ask me. This enternet is not enough to answer all your questions."

"Internet." She corrected him. "Right, I have a question for you Abdus. Oh! Sorry, Ashwatthama! What would you like to be referred to?"

"Abeedah please listen to me. You can call me whatever you want. I am still your Abdus! A name doesn't define me. I will always be if you'll have me. Ashwatthama is my past, but you're my future. Please try to understand."

"Understand? That is so easy for you to say…. Tell me. I want to know now!"

"I am an immortal. It has been more than 5000 years I have been residing in different parts of the world. Not residing, more precisely, I have been paying for my sins. "

"Immortal? But you don't look old?" She asked.

"My ageing process is too slow to be noticed."

"It says, I mean it's written on the internet that you are cursed?"

"Yes. I am not a good human. I have committed some grave sins in my life which I wish I shouldn't have done. I was one of the warriors in Mahabharata. Dronacharya, my father, was a noble teacher for Kauravas and Pandavas." He replied looking at Abeedah's terrified face.

After a long pause, he continued, "Initially, my father was a poor Brahmin. We didn't have a single cow in spite of belonging to such a respectable class of the society. During those days I was a child. Because we were so poor, I had never even tasted milk. I used to play with other Brahmin children and they all used to drink milk, always shared their joy of having it.

My mother would give me a mixture of rice flour and water and I recognized that mix as milk. My mother did this because she never wanted to make me feel inferior. But the truth was that I was still deprived of the taste of real milk. I craved it so much that I meditated for six month to please Lord Shiva who then gave me milk. My parents loved me way beyond their limitations, and this love became the reason for their death.

My father felt very sad, and he went to his old friend, Drupada, to ask for a cow for his son. Drupada refused for it. At that moment, my father vowed to take revenge from Drupada. He promised himself to provide a better life for his son and family.

Time passed, and he became the royal teacher to train the princes of Hastinapur. He gave me everything. He gave me his name, unconditional love, and a good life. For him, I favored Kauravas in the battle of Mahabharata. It was said that the battle was fought for the establishment and reinforcement of Dharma." Abdus stood up and went to the window.

"I was its witness, Abeedah and it was never for Dharma! It was a bloodbath, and thousands of lives were lost to satisfy self-esteem of a man whose ego wouldn't permit him to admit that it was wrong on his part to insult a woman in front of everyone. False pride of men who were supposedly the most powerful or the biggest archer or most righteous, but stayed quiet throughout when their wife, their daughter-in-law, was begging for help!

My father was extremely talented, knowledgeable and blessed with spiritual powers. Pandavas faced huge difficulty in defeating my father during the war. It was the fifteenth day of the war when Duryodhana charged my father as a traitor. My father got instigated, and in anger, he tried to use the Brahmadanda weapon. This divine weapon had the power of the Saptrishi. It was way more potent than the Brahmastra. My father had never imparted the knowledge of this holy weapon to neither to me nor to his favorite student, Arjuna.

Meanwhile, Brahma came to the rescue and asked him to take his weapon back. Later it turned out that my father could never be defeated. It was crucial for the Pandavas to kill my father to win this war. More subsequently, Vasudev suggested tricking my father. Yudhishthira, the righteous brother amongst the Pandavas, made a false claim for first the time in his life. He lied that I was dead."

"He lied to kill your father?" Abeedah asked. All this while, she had beenpatiently listening to Abdus.

"Yes. It was a filthy strategy. Ashwatthama was killed, but it was an 'Elephant' named as Ashwatthama. They killed an elephant called Ashwatthama and delivered that news to my father. It was all a game of words. My father used to trust Yudhishthira blindly, and he ultimately forgot that his son was blessed with immortality. He gave up his arms and was killed by Drushtadyumna." He said.

"Who was Drushtadyumna?" She asked.

"He was Pandavas brother-in-law," he explained.

"Their brother-in-law. How many sisters this guy had? " She asked curiously.

Abdus chucked and said, "One sister. Her name was Draupadi, who was the wife of Pandavas which means a wife of all five brothers."

"You mean five husbands of one woman, all living together in harmony under the same roof?" Abeedah made weird face with an awkward chuckle, "I mean it is really hard to imagine." This was one of her quality to find human in everything. She was getting herself settled into the story. Now she was not afraid of Abdus.

"It's a complicated story." He replied.

"What happened then? And how you end up in that forest?" she asked curiously.

"I was trained in advanced military arts. I was highly capable of being a chief commander, but I was approached by Duryodhana when the war had officially ended, and only three Kauravas were left. I favored him in this battle though I was aware that it was the side of Adharma.

Abeedah interrupted him, "Then why did you do it? Why did you fight along with them?"

He sighed, "Being a servant of Hastinapur and crowned king of Panchal, I was bound to fight for the Kauravas. I even tried to guide Duryodhana to hold treaty or a peace agreement after the death of Dushasana, but he didn't agree."

He sighed, now his voice really heavy, "To take revenge against Pandavas for killing my father deceitfully and as promised to Duryodhana, I, along with my uncle and a friend, Kritverma attacked the camp of Pandavas at midnight. I had worshipped Shiva, and He granted a boon that whoever would come across my path that night would die by my Chandrahaas sword, which was gifted to Ravana by the God himself.

While attacking, I killed Dhristidymna and ended up killing the five sons of the Pandavas erroneously and. It was" He felt ashamed to continue. He lowered his head facing the floor. He was facing difficulty to maintain his eye contact with Abeedah. At the same time, he was not weak enough to withstand Abeedah's reaction to this fact.

"What happened then?" She asked in a low and hesitant voice.

"I took their heads to Duryodhana and when with delightful eyes Duryodhana looks at those heads, his face turned to disappointment because he knew it is of the young ones of Draupadi and not that of his cousins. Duryodhana asks me to seek advice from sage Vedvyasa. So, when I went to the hermitage of the sage, I found Pandavas were already up there along with Vasudev to avenge their sons' death. I was supposed to accept my wrong doings in the hermitage, and sought help from Lord Krishna or Sage Vyasa and penance for my sins but, instead I was captured. They wanted revenge so I fought them. I enchanted a straw of Hay at the Pandavas after reciting the Brahmastra mantra into it. Arjuna, my father's favorite student, his prodigy, in return, also invoked the same weapon. It had the power to destroy the world. Due to this fear, Maharishi Vyasa advised both of us to summon back our weapons. Arjuna withdrew it, but I was unable to do the same.

Unfortunately, I only knew invoking the weapon. I never knew how to revoke it. I decided to choose a soft target and directed the weapon towards the womb of a pregnant lady, Uttara, Arjuna's daughter-in-law. This decision led to the death of the fetus of Uttara which eventually killed the only heir of the Pandavas. This was the whole brutal and shameful act done by me."

A loud gasp escaped Abeedah before she could help herself. She could not believe her sweet Abdus, who took Ryan to the fair to please him despite his hate for the crowds, could do such a heinous thing.

Abdus smiled sadly, "My father's death destroyed my compassion and mental health. I was blind enough to remain loyal towards the underserved ones.

After this heinous act, I deserved punishment. I was asked to surrender my forehead gem, the one that granted me strength and immortality, and then Vasudev cursed me to forever suffer deep wounds on my forehead and body. Such wounds would never get healed till I am breathing. I was cursed to stay alone and deprived of love forever. Days passed, years passed, even centuries passed. I was breathing, but I died on that day itself when I was cursed."

"You mean to say, everything was real, Gods, war, demons, supernatural weapons, they existed? Still exist?"

"Yes, everything is true. In fact, I standing in front of you prove it. It's all true." He replied.

"I thought they were just stories or lore, passed on from generation to generations. We use to play those characters and perform those plays. But never believed it was real. What happened then?" Abeedah said in a surprised voice.

"Since then I have been wandering. I have visited different parts of the world. Every second, every moment of my life, I was paying off my sins. My pain was beyond the limit of a rational human being's suffering. We all can endure physical pain, but I have been experiencing a deep mental pain. I begged, I literally asked several times to liberate me and grant me death, but Vasudev never responded.

After returning the blood thirsty sword of Mahakaal where it belonged, I went to the one place where I always found peace as a child, the place which was pilgrim for my ascetic father, where he received the knowledge of archery from Lord Shiva.

Thinking once again I will find peace and Mahadev would hear to my plea. I did penance for a centuries, but this time Shiva was standing with Vasudev against me, he never showed up.

Gradually, I started accepting and enduring my pain. I accepted this fact that it is better to make peace with the inevitable. I have seen this world-changing its velocity, its appearance and its time. I always led a secluded life. For my survival, I used to hunt animals and survived on wild fruits. I was a warrior, and I never had any other option apart from using its skills. I quickly learned to use the weapons, and I was shocked to notice I was even getting paid for my teachings.

After completing my penance, when I came out of the cave, the world was all together different place. I was depressed, devastated and alone with no motive in life, the only thing I had was an endless time.

Since then finding a cure to my curse was the only goal in my life. I was there when the old civilization were emerging. I marched different countries in search of a cure but everything I tried was just temporary healing. Then I met the most generous people and found a little drop of peace with Indians. You may know them as Native Americans. They treated me as their own and the way they had a bond with nature was impressive. It was liberating, that they just accepted me as I was. I didn't have to hide my immortality with them.

They could talk and understand the element of nature. They gave me a shelter and in return I gave them my knowledge of archery and self protection techniques. Many centuries passed with then in a blink of an eye.

One night when everyone was sleeping and dreaming with their loved ones at their wigwam homes, I woke up with the smell of burn. When I came out of my hut, I saw a house was burning with large flames; I jumped inside to check and found a two year old boy, who wouldn't stop crying. His name was Nituna. I saved him but couldn't save his parents, who were dead already.

With no time, everyone panicked and started running to the nearby lake to fetch water. After the fire was brought under control, the chief with two of his brave men dragged those two dead bodies outside

I adopted him and raised him as my own. I formed a kinship with him as we both were orphans, alone in the world. I loved him like my own son and he respected me like a father. I raised him the way my father raised me, like a warrior and loved him just like my mother loved me. I was his whole world and he was mine. He grew inches to ages in from of me while I remained the same. From a two year old innocent child to a young warrior, and from a young warrior to an old chief of the tribe, I watched him at every stage and at last I saw him counting his last days too.

For me watching him die was something that was beyond my strength. But I never wished to exchange my life with his death, because death was far better to accept then the immortality.

The only decision I had in my hand was to leave him as watching him die something I could never prepare myself for. I left him and left the colony without any words. Nituna, has always been and will always have a special place in my heart and memories. Whenever I am with Manik, I feel the presence of Nituna around me.

Again, I was alone wondering in the world on my feet and again I found a rich culture in Egypt. I worked as a labor for many years and then marched for the next place. I this was only I kept my identity secret and spirit high.

I had been a part of world famous wars but all in disguise. Fought many wars for many kings protecting their kingdom and later, for countries protecting their freedom because of a warrior, all I was. Everyone knew me in spite of being an outsider. I was easily selected for the first rankers in the army because of my size and skills. I was tallest and best of them all."

"Why am I not surprised?" Abeedah muttered.

"Initially I saw it as an opportunity to lift up my spirit. But the bloodbath and the brutal outcome made me re-live the Kurukshetra war, every day and when it became unbearable. I left fighting and never lifted any weapon again.

Again centuries passed, the world took its leap, and I saw a new era spreading around. People fought fewer wars and peace was being promoted. Gradually, this concept of war faded and my quality of warrior was of no use. I was again living an aimless life. After world wars, I retreated back to forests.

Then, I started wandering in the forests again. And that is why you found me in that condition in that forest. After wondering for decades, I ended up in the first where you found me and my body became weak and the wounds became more painful. I had no other option to make those caves my home. I was there for more than couple of decades. I had almost given up, and then you came to my life like a beam of hope."

"This was quite short story to cover 5000 years", Abeedah folded her hands like some teacher, as she never missed a chance to put a counter question.

"Honestly, I don't have any problem to give you every single details of every single year. I have all the time in the world but for you every single day counts. Although, I am not a story teller, these are the most of the words, I have used in centuries." Abdus replied holding her little finger.

It was almost morning when Abdus completed his story. He stood up and went near the window. It was indeed too much for Abeedah, but she could understand his pain. She went near the window and held his hand. "It has been a never-ending suffering for me until you came in my life.

My wounds started healing since you touched them and my soul has started breathing. You are my world, dear. I would never hurt you Abeedah. I love you and would do even if you ask me to leave you right now." He tried to control his tears.

Abeedah smiled. She said with calmness in her eyes, "It's true that whatever you did was wrong. Indeed you have suffered a lot, and I feel you have paid your debt. I won't let you suffer anymore. Just give me some time to settle into tour story, make peace with who you are."

She went to the window and hugged his back. Abdus turned and enveloped her in his arms, pressing a soft kiss to her temples.

"Although I still have one question!" she asked.

"Of course you do."

"If your name is Ashwatthama, what is the story behind Abdus Samad?"

"Once I was wandering near the East. It was more of a desert. On my way, I met a blind Prophet who asked me to help him to walk few miles. He seemed thirsty and tired of marching for days but had no signs of stress on his face. He was calmer than a resting lake. I held his hand to support him. He asked my name, but I refused to answer.

No sooner I touched him; he looked straight into my eyes, his pupils were completely diluted, but he could see through me. He gave a weird smile as if he had discovered a treasure. Then he called me Abdus Samad. Throughout the journey, he called me Abdus Samad. So when you were asking my name, this name came to my mind." He winked with a smile.

"What does this 'Abdus Samad' mean?"

He took a pause, scratched his head then with a deep sigh replied, "It means 'The Servant of Eternal'. I guess he was supernatural and he was aware of my story."

"Oh! Now I understand that why you had thrown that lion's statue on the idol of Krishna. But Abdus, that was wrong on your part. You can show your discontentment to him, but the way you have reflected was not acceptable in any manner. That status is not only a statue, but he is people's belief now.

Everyone wants to believe in their existence; they want to believe that the sadness in their life will soon be swallowed with happiness, they want to believe that their existence has a meaning and those idols, GODS provides them those beliefs. Religion makes it easier to deal with all the random, hard to bear shitty things that happen to us, humans. You did not only break that ideal you tried to Sabotage their beliefs." She said.

"I understand that. You won't believe how much I have cursed myself for this. I am sorry".

After a brief moment of silence and a cup of coffee, Abeedah asked, "Can I ask you one more thing?"

"I am afraid you are going to, anyway."

Abeedah with a apologetic expression in her face said, "Though I don't know much about Hindu mythology but I knew about Lord Krishna, I knew about Pandavas and I also heard about some other warriors name. Either in story books or skit we played in school but I never heard about you."

"Well, look at me, if they would've focused on me, nobody would've remembered others." He chuckled. Then he answered somberly, "I do not have answer to this Abeedah. I guess people have a tendency to forget the undesirables and so did history. Maybe I wasn't worth remembering. Or maybe it was also a part of my curse." He replied hiding his sadness behind the smile.

"Rubbish. You are worth remembering. You are worth everything. Okay now. Enough of your story, I have had enough. I have something important to tell you" Abeedah said in an exciting tone.

"After such a heavy discussion, how you are so excited?" he was surprised.

She knelt down and asked Abdus to follow her posture. She held his hands and said, "Abdus… yes, you are still my Abdus, and I would always call you by this name. You were right. Ashwatthama was your past, and I can see the repentance in your character, in your eyes, in your words, in your actions! I don't know whether Vasudev will ever forgive you, but I am forgiving you and liberating you from all your deeds. You have all the right to live your life as you want to and you will be loved forever. Trust me. "

As they were caught up in the story, the door bell rang. Abeedah answered the door and saw Mr. Tawde standing with the same news on the television. The news has already spread to Abeedah's building and Mr. Tawde was there to warn Abeedah about the man in the news whose description was similar to Abdus.

He kept all the words in his mouth and started spilling it as she opened the door, "Abeedah, I saw a video in the news about the person who broke—."

Before he could complete his sentence, looking at Abeedah's face he sensed that Abdus was the culprit and his old bone went cold. He took a step backwards and said point at Abdus, "It was you, right?"

He shaky legs tried to move as fast as they could and went to the elevator and started pressing the button continuously. Abeedah followed Mr. Tawde to the lift and tried to explain, more like deny the fact that it was Abdus who started the mess. No sooner, Abdus also reach to them but by the time he reached, Mr. Tawde went inside the elevator, ignoring Abeedah's requests. To her mind it was the end of Abdus in her life, and for the first time she truly understood the reason behind him hiding behind the wood, away from mankind, amongst animals and birds but universe was still not sure of their separation now.

Mr. Tawde entered the elevator car and his sweater got stuck as the doors and while it started moving to the ground floor, he started banging the door hard shouting, "Help! Help!."

Abdus asked Abeedah to step back; he put his hands in the middle of the door and started pushing it apart, the automatic doors was not that easy to be opened, even for Ashwatthama. He put all his power, which could be easily visible on his bulging veins and pushed it harder. Although he opened the door but new age machines are not programmed to fail easily. The external pressure short-circuited the elevator mechanism and an unexpected malfunction took place, breaking the tension wire which made it fall speedily to the ground with Mr. Tawde inside it. The car hit the floor hard enough to take old Mr. Tawde's life.

With the last breath on his lungs and a secret buried inside his heart, he was dead. Once again, Abdus was a victim of unintended crime and blood in his hand but for Abeedah, it was an unending series of death bodies.

After a brief moment of grief, she realised that if Mr. Tawde could identify Abdus, then somebody could also recognise him from the video.

Due to the crowd and police enquiring about Mr.Tawde's accident, Abdus could not get out of the building. She asked him to hide under the kitchen storage for the night, until she figures out a way to get him out of the building.

One more night was added for her to go sleepless and worried. But she somehow managed to close her eyes for an hour or two when she woke up at noise of alarm clock. Worried sick to her stomach, she went to the drawing room and switch on the News channel to know the live situation of the city, under the riot.

But was shocked to hear the news, "The man behind the sinister, behind the raising anger of the country has surrendered himself. He has the same appearance as the man in the video and he took the full responsibility for the Krishna temple incident. But he refuse to give any reason for his misdeed."

Though, it was difficult for both of them to understand the reason behind an unknown man suddenly showing up and confessing for the things, he didn't even do. But it also made a room for relief for them.

She kept being all the things that happened and started getting ready for the work when she heard the door bell again. She stood near the door while it rang many time, guessing and skeptical about the person standing outside and the motive.

Abdus saw her getting cold feet to open the door. He volunteered and opened it up for her. She took a deep relaxing breath sing the post man holding a parcel for her.

She smiled. After signing the delivery she sat on the sofa and checked the parcel. It was a nondescript parcel about the size of a chocolate box with no return address. She opened it, and had the contents out which were the least expected things she would've imagined to be inside the parcel.

They were authentic passport and identity proof documents in the name of Abdus Samad. They both looked at each other with a question mark on their faces. Who would have gone this length to make authentic documents for Abdus, when nobody knew about him?

The last question that grabbed both of their minds but never came out was, "Is the same person who sent these documents is behind the imposter of Abdus, any who the incidence was an erupted lava which could destroy everything, instead went cold with a splash of water?"

Chapter twelve

Marriage isn't easy

One year later...

Before marriage, all that is important is love and respect between two persons. But after marriage, comes the living together and that mean learning everything about their partners. A year passed like a ship floating in the sea, which goes passes through many waves some small some high enough to make it struggle, but it reaches the shore no matter how hard it is. This year was a very new experience for Abdus; it was his first step to a marital life which was full of ups and downs which was always tasted spicy with the little addition of drama.

No matter if a woman gets a man of his dreams or settles down in marriage, she will still be able to pick up the flaws and shortcomings. No matter how happy they are little fights will always act as the cherry at the top of the cake. In this case, the cake is marriage.

What Abdus didn't know was that, Abeedah was cleanliness freak. Their bedroom wall painted with the lighter shade of purple. She had everything from bed sheets to curtain, from carpet to the bean bag everything matching to the wall colour. No matter how many times she stood up from the bed, she had this habit of removing the crease from the sheet, wiping it off.

Abeedah and Abdus were also going through the same graph of life. Their morning started with a cup of coffee and newspaper for Abeedah, but Abdus was still couldn't get enough of the technology.

Abdus's morning started with coffee and television, which led by Abeedah shouting at him for the wet towel on the bed and Abdus apologizing with a kiss on her cheek. But he repeated it every morning just as an excuse to kiss her.

Abdus still had his royal habits as well as untidiness from his cave days, which sometimes pissed uptight Abeedah. At least twice a month she figuratively killed him with her silence because of the broken lamp on his side of the bed. Abdus's hands were long and strong, which made him break the night lamp now and then in his sleep whenever he the same dream in which he punched someone.

Next morning Abeedah would know he had the same dream when she sees the scattered piece of the lamp on the floor, but she couldn't help her anger, but it was just useless to yell on him as he never did it purposely. She always wondered who the person he always fights in his dreams was, but Abdus never revealed the enemy in his dream. In return, Abeedah gave him, her silent treatment which always ended with Abeedah's barely concealed smile after hearing Abdus's line, "When will you realise that I am a great catch?"

By now Abdus had also learned to humor his life from Abeedah, which many times back failed too. But Abdus knew her very well, every day their love grew stronger and stronger along with their little disagreement discussions and annoying habits.

But he was undoubtedly enjoying the new role of being husband.

It was his second year in this technically advanced world. Every day he felt privileges to be surrounded by such amazing things. He never knew what to watch as there were so many options. He had crossed almost half the globe, so he never found travel shows much of interest. The daily drama shows were like a sitcom to him. But being a foodie, he loved to watch cooking shows a lot. He always felt amazed at television even if there was nothing of his interest on it; he just set on the couch changing the channels.

One day, Abdus comes into the room after watching the television sees Abeedah on the bed on her cotton pajama and t-shirt waiting for him, reading a book.

"What are you reading?"

"A Tale of two cities. When I was passing by the railway station, I saw this book. It is quite famous just wanted to know what the fuzz is all about. Apart from that I really liked the cover." She replied showing him the cover of the book.

"AH. I like this book too" Abdus replied in the excitement which he always does whenever he found any common ground or interests in their lives. Otherwise, they mostly had north, south opinion about almost everything.

"I like it so far, but it's a little dark for my taste."

"Well, it is Charles Dickens. The French revolution was a dark period. What did you expect?" he shrugged.

"You say as if you were there," Abeedah said while preparing herself for comfortable sleep by fluffing the pillow on her side.

"Well, Yes, I was there."

"No! You're joking right?" her eyes popped from the drowsy state.

"Why would I lie? I told you I roamed around the world. Because there was not much for me, So, I kept myself busy in trying to heal my wounds."

"Yeah, that's all you've told me." Abeedah said irritation laced in her voice. A year before, when he told her his secrets he told her a lot of thing, but still they hadn't talked more about his past anymore than what he revealed that night.

"What else do you want to know? Imagine reading a huge pile of history books. My life is like that."

"Well, I'd like a history lesson from my very handsome husband."

After such insistence, how could he deny her? He started telling the story, "Well, India was a big exporter of fabrics, muslin, spices and traders came to India, so I traveled with them, first to Mesopotamia and from there I never stopped, I traveled a lot, from places to places. I was in Europe in the 19th century. Dickens was right. It was the best of times for the bourgeoisie and worst of the times for proletariats."

"Wow. I have an encyclopedia as a husband." Enthusiastically she said, "Tell me more."

"France is a beautiful city, right? I love European architecture. Victorian dresses. What did you do there?" She was curious to know about his past. Therefore, she never led any moment to skip where she could learn about him.

"Well at the time, it wasn't. You should be happy that you can enjoy vintage things while having Phones, wifi, and human rights. There were poor people everywhere. I lived among them"

"How did you feel living there?" She asked, given that Abdus lived his life as a royalty.

"Well, you would expect me, a royal, to react poorly to the poverty and lack of food and bad living conditions. But surprisingly, I had seen worse things. I have already told you that I grew up dirt poor. We didn't have much growing but we had love."

He looked back at her with a smirk on his face, but then grew somber as he continued, "My point is that, I just wanted to heal. So how I lived didn't matter. When you live in poverty, you realise the actual importance of life because every single they struggle to live, they struggle to survive, they struggle to fight the cold. For rich people, they just pass by the day, but when I lived with them, I saw them sleeping in peace because they survived that day." Abdus replied like he was talking about weather.

"You witnessed many deaths and pain around you. How could you be so cavalier about it? It doesn't seem like you have an iota of emotion about this." Abeedah asked incredulously.

He stood up, irritation evident his voice, "Abeedah I have seen horrors one cannot imagine. I don't feel very sympathetic towards humankind, you know why? Because we are the worst things that has happened to earth. History is violent, it's the truth. It may not affect one to read about it in books, but to see it? Live amongst the chaos? It's the stuff nightmare are made of. Do you want to know the wars I have faced?"

"Yes, tell me. That's all I have been asking you all this time. I want to know what you have seen. What you have suffered."

He sighed," I was in China when the First world war happened. They did not directly participate, but in some ways they did. There were Chinese traders all around the world. I heard about some ancient Chinese techniques that help to heal. At first, I thought that it was stupid to seek it. If our Indian medicines couldn't help, what will Chinese do? But I was desperate. So I went there. They taught me about different meditation techniques, calming my mind is necessary, they said. I learned a lot.

Even the most peaceful land hit the disaster with my footsteps on it. A terrible earthquake happened in a town; I went to help them. Pulled out few people, treated them. I was still in China when 2nd world war started. And I was still sick, had wounds over my body, still desperate to heal. There were German troops in China as they were getting help from Germany to fight Japan. I was working as s stable boy who used to tend to animals. One day I heard from one of the German soldiers about this person called Bruno Gröning. Apparently, he was a healer of divine powers and could heal anyone.

I was already getting attached to China and people there, and I decided it was time to move on. I joined the soldiers and hid and reached Germany. Just my luck, the guy was a sham and could not help me. I had to survive and live somehow, so I stayed in Germany, which brought me face to face with another cruelty, which never made any sense to me. They were herding Jews like animals in trains to send them to extermination camps."

He stood up and went to the window looking out. His jaw was tight and closed his eyes. He took a deep breath and continued with pain in his voice, "Abeedah, there were children, women, innocent people, pushed into gas chambers. It was murder, Abeedah, stone cold mass murder. I can still remember the look on the faces of those poor souls. You know what their fault was? Their religion, their faith. It was horrible. Even though I had seen slavery and how those whites treated the people of colour. Hell, I was on the receiving end of such behaviours too many times to count, but they usually backed away because of my size and power. Anyone rarely saw me as I covered my body with cloaks and clothes to hide my wounds. But that incident notably stayed with me. I felt ashamed that such atrocities were happening in front of me and all I was concerned was healing my cursed body. That's why I came back here, fought in the wars. I remember the speech of independence on the radio at midnight. I remember the division of the country. People were leaving their homes and families and fighting and killing in the name of religion. I had lost hope. Had lost trust in humanity and hoped that I would ever heal. It was not just a curse to live forever with a broken body."

He turned to look at her, "The curse was to see things happening in the world, even today, and see the worst of humanity and still live among them. To live hopelessly. I couldn't take it anymore, so I retreated to the caves and lived there. Alone, in despair, without hope. Until I met you, Abeedah. You are not just my love and my wife. You are my hope. My reason to live this cursed life. My joy, my everything. You saved me. You not only healed my body but you treated my heart and my mind, my conscious."

Abdus sighed in disappointment after hearing the story out loud from his own mouth he said, "You know Abeedah, sometimes I feel that through our time did not have this technologies but it was a pure and straightforward time. Though we had our sins, at-least we fought for what we could get, not for what people are born with. At least everybody got a fair chance to fight for what they want. I have seen people being killed for their skin colour, for their beliefs, for their religion and it was not at all humanely. It was brutal even for me. Every evening after the battle, post-sunset we paid our condolences to all the warrior who lost their lives fighting, no matter for which clan they fought they were cremated together. That is not the case anymore."

Unable to stand Abeedah's silence anymore, he went and hugged Abeedah tightly, "Please say something."

"I don't know what to say Abdus, I understand why you thing how you think given what you have witnessed, but I want you to not lose hope. At least not now, that we're together."

He looked at her and held her face in his palms, kissing her chastely on her lips, "I promise I'll try."

Later after they went to bed, Abeedah couldn't sleep. Whole night Abeedah kept on thinking, how strange their lives were. She had a husband about whom she knew nothing apart from what he told. He has lived more than a hundred lives and how she knew just a small fraction of it. Being a woman many thoughts occurred in her minds filled with doubts and confusion, especially after hearing the story of Nituna.

What if she is just like a visitor to him? She might live 30-40 years together but what is the value of these times for him. For her, Abdus was his life, but she can't even expect the same from him. She knew she would take her last breathe with him. But for Abdus this time was just like another bucket of water in the sea.

For the first time after their marriage, she realised the fact that he is immortal. What would happen after 20 years when people will question about his aging, or lack of thereof? He will look the same as he is now and she will be a turning to an old lady. She turned towards Abdus and glazed at his sleeping face and realized how much she loved him. She got sick to her stomach thinking of him with somebody else after her death. She made many predictions of his life after her. He was handsome as hell, kind-hearted, brave and above all, he had this undeniable great personality. But this was something she had no control over.

She wanted to sleep, but the rambling thoughts kept her awake. She concluded her thoughts by making herself a promise that she will make each day count and love him as much as she could, so that no woman could take her place in future, that no woman would be good enough for him.

Between her terrifying thoughts of the reality, the most significant dilemma for her was to decide. Which character she related the most Wendy of Peter Pan from Neverland or Bella of Edward from Twilight? That night she watched both the movies back to back, to figure out the answer.

Next morning she kept her promise. She got up before Abdus, because she didn't sleep the whole night which doesn't usually happen and made his favorite breakfast in bed. Abdus was not much surprised with her gesture but was happy. They had the morning breakfast together, and as they finished, Abdus started picking up the crumbs on the bone china and picked up his plate.

Abeedah snatched the plate from his hand and asked him to relax. She kept the plate on the side table and started making out with him. Now Abdus suspected her strange behavior because Abeedah never liked morning romance.

He asked her "What is happening, here?"

"What do you mean, Am I not allow to love my husband, do I have to take permission for this?"

Abdus felt insane for doubting her and enjoyed the moment. After a little romance Abdus went to take a bath and following the daily habits, he left the wet towel on the bed. Abeedah after packing her's and Abdus's lunch, came to the bedroom to get ready for the hospital and something unexpected happened. Without yelling at him for throwing the wet towel on the bed, she picked it up and kept in the laundry basket. Now Abdus was sure that something was up. Something was cooking inside of her.

Abdus urged her to answer what was going on. Then Abeedah started revealing her concerns, "The thing is, last night I couldn't sleep at all after hearing your story."

"Why? Was there something I shouldn't have said?"

"Oh No, I just…I just left out of your life."

"What do you mean?"

"I always knew that you are immortal but last night it blew me in my face. I realized that you had lived so long that I don't know anything about it. Above all, I realized the fact that you will live a long life even after me."

"So, what difference does it makes?"

"I mean what if you forget me and forget I ever existed or I might just be a part of your stories like the one you told me yesterday. I just couldn't bear such thoughts."

"So you are getting jealous of the girl who is not even born yet."

Abeedah made a confused and disgusted face and asked. "What?"

"I mean you will be with me for thirty or forty years. Ok, let's take best case scenario fifty years. Then only I will be with some other person. So, don't expect me to find a fifty year old wrinkly woman. I mean look at me, I deserve better than that." He said humorously and laughed hard looking at Abeedah's disgusted face. Of course, even after almost two years with Abeedah, Abdus still did not have much experience with women's emotional swings.

So, to change her thoughts and to make her laugh, he made the most outrageous comment. After hearing which Abeedah drew with anger and disappointment left the room. It was that moment Abdus realized he had made the stupidest mistake and followed her to the kitchen.

In a rush to reach her and make a amends with her, he tripped and in order to steady himself, he pushed something that broke as it hit the ground. First the lamp then the frame hanging on the wall in the drawing room which she loved the most. It had their marriage picture.

With the sound, Abeedah turned back and saw the frame on the floor, broken. A girl will always find a way to show her anger with little drama, "Thank you for breaking the frame. I knew it doesn't matter to you how important this is for me. Now do me a favor and throw it outside."

"Abeedah it was just a mistake, I didn't mean to break it and what I said was not true. It was just to change your mood and make you laugh."

"Laugh? You wanted me to laugh after putting my heart out to you."

Abdus had no idea how she turned his words again him. But he was persuasive; he didn't stop "I love you Abeedah, nobody else."

"For now right?"

Abdus realised he had made a big mistake and no matter what he says in defense, it will be used against him. It was better to surrender than to fight "No, always. There was no one before you, and there will be no one after you."

"My death is not in my hand, but the person whom I choose to love forever is. And I have already chosen you."

Abeedah's anger vanished at that instance. She said, "But you are immortal, and I am not. Every girl wants to grow old with her life partner, but I don't have that option either. It is not like you are a vampire, who will bite me and make me immortal too. Are you?"

Abdus laughed hard at her solutions and said, "See this is what I expected when I made that joke."

"What joke?" she asked.

"The joke about…", He stopped immediately. Abeedah knew which so-called joke he was talking about. Knowing that this was a trick in which cannot fall again. It will be like poking the bear again. He thought to himself "Why woman makes everything so complicated and why it is so hard to argue with them."

"Abeedah trust me you don't have anything to worry about."

Abeedah knew Abdus for more than a couple of years now, and she knew him well enough to understand that he was a difficult person to convince of anything. He had built a solid wall as a barrier between his present and past which was very difficult to break down or even to peek through it. But one cannot connect to the person knowing only one phase of life. Surely not when they have vowed to be each other's life partner.

Abeedah opted a strategy to make him understand what she wanted. She smiled at him to deliberately tell him that they were at a stand, and then she said, "Our home is so beautiful, cozy and safe. Isn't it?"

"Yes, it is," Abdus replied although he knew the question was not just a generic question but some strategy to make her point, which he knew but deliberately tried to dodge all these years. But female species are smart and an advent one. When they want something, they surely knew how to get it. Also, they are great politicians; they know how to get what they want in a 3way that it will be delivered to them self willingly. Therefore, many great wars were fought for them and many undefeatable legendary heroes of the history sacrificed their lives either to prove their love or to protect the respect of a woman.

Abeedah asked him to open the window in the drawing room. Abdus nodded and walked towards the window, but with every step, he took towards he was waiting like the ticking clock for the catch, the whole point of this little skit she was playing. He unlocked the window and pushed both the doors of outside. It was the end of rainy season, and the wooden frame had expanded significantly which made a weird creaking sound like opening the doors of an old chamber.

Abeedah waited for a couple of seconds, expecting any question coming from him, because the window hadn't had been opened the whole winter. But she saw no words coming out of him.

She signed and continued, "Sometimes this house makes me nauseous when all windows are closed it feels suffocating. It's like living in the box without any contact with the world. And that's what I feel sometimes living with you."

Abdus murmured to himself facing towards the window, "Here it comes."

She continues while cleaning the dishes and keeping the plates on the shelf, "When I don't know any phase of your life apart from what I see now. And this feeling will never go until you open the windows inside of you, which you have sealed so tightly."

Abdus played the last card he had in his mind to change the topic of conversation; he said, "Do you remember tomorrow is our first marriage anniversary?"

"Oh thank God! You at least remember that." She taunted him and went to their bedroom. When she came out of the room, she was holding a big box wrapped in multi-colored glitter paper with a big bow tied around it. It was an anniversary gift she had for him. She kept the gift on the table and said in a pissed manner, "I am in no mood to celebrate it now."

"It is so thoughtful of you, Abeedah. Thank you." He said but received a cold nod in return from her.

Abdus sat on the couch and opened the gift. Abeedah had gifted him a gramophone and some record collection of Jazz music. She knew how much Abdus loved this genre of music. Many times, they used to dance together in some numbers, or she could hear him singing along with the music. This time he knew there was no way to get out of the situation. It was clearly visible to him, her adamancy to get what she wanted from him.

"What do want for a gift from me?"

"Yeah, as if I will really get what I want."

"Anything, you say."

Abeedah's sullen face was replaced with a devilish smile. Finally, her little act paid off. He got to hear what she wanted. She kept the last plate on the shelf and turned towards him like any Bollywood movie actress when she heard the news has been waiting for.

"I want to see your past."

After taking couple of deep breathes he said, "Okay then, and pack your bags. We are going on our second honeymoon tomorrow."

Abdus already knew what he was dealing with and where this conversation was going. He was ashamed of his deed that he always kept it hidden from her. Although, after many centuries he was left with nothing but only one thing from his past, but now he was ready to face his fear. To meet the only piece of his history, he was soon able to come face-to-face with his sin and guilt.

He had told Abeedah a gist of it but to reveal it completely? To show her the one thing that was a souvenir of his sin, his brutality, his guilt. Though he was doing this for Abeedah, but he himself needed to break the shield he created to overcome his fear. The fear which was killing him bit by bit inside. The fear which still could shallow his happiness.

Chapter thirteen

Chandrahaas Sword

It was a very early direct flight to Delhi, then an hour and a half drive to Greater Noida. Abeedah was all packed and excited that her night felt like summer season, longest and moving in slow motion. They reached the airport with a swollen face and dull eyes. Abdus never missed a chance to take his power nap, on the other hand, it was Abeedah's first chance to meet his husband's mysterious past, was geared up.

As the flight took off Abdus again went back to his nap time while Abeedah starred out the dark window with was slowly turning brighter and brighter. After an hour, sun finally woke up and started his job. It was for the first time she saw the sun rise above the cloud which had all shades of red and there could be nothing more soothing and watched the colors in the sky mixing into itself.

Without any delay in landing, they touched the ground in exactly two hours. Abeedah patted Abdus to wake him up. Abdus in his typical manner stretched his arms carefree, for which he ended up apologizing to the next seat passenger who had the most dreadful expression throughout the journey.

Abdus whispered in Abeedah's ears point his thumb towards his neighbor, "Why the man looks so annoyed?"

Abeedah whispered back, "Because you kept you large hands resting on the handles. He had to scoot himself the whole time."

Abdus showed his teeth to give him an apologizing smile and stood up from his seat. As he tried to shrink himself to cross the passenger seat, his heavy foot stepped over the man. Abdus though now the man was so pissed that he won't take his apology for the third time. So he decided not to look at him and moved towards the exit door as fast as he could. Abeedah found the whole scenario hilarious.

The moment they came out of the airport. There was number of taxi drivers offering them their service that it was hard for them to choose one. From the crowd a taxi driver came up to them and said in his weird accent mixed with his native language, "Sir, I will take you anywhere you want in cheap. I have a new car. It will be very comfortable I promise."

The accent suddenly struck Abeedah. She knew this accent. She recalled Chagan from their trip to Chhattisgarh had the same accent.

She asked the driver,"Are you from Chhattisgarh?"

"Yes, madam" he replied.

Abdus saw the look on Abeedah's face as if she had a flashback going on in his mind. He knew what exactly was going on in his mind. The accent was attached to a trip which completely changed her life. Without wasting any time they hopped on the SUV and started their two hours journey to Bisrakh. Abdus couldn't ignore the excitement on Abeedah's face and said, "Last time I saw this place was a small town with a handful of people living in. The Place is nothing of any excitement. Don't get your hopes high."

"I am not excited to visit the temple, but I am excited to see the only piece of your past that you've held back." She replied.

Even in this excitement, the driver's accent brought back her horrifying memories of the trip which she cannot forget. The last moments of her with Shad and Ragini made her sad. She couldn't hide her mixed emotion.

Abdus saw her lost in her thoughts. An hour passed but she was still floating in the memories which she buried deep inside her. It was like opening a forbidden chamber after a long time. At a point, Abdus saw her wet eyes without any tear shredding beneath that. Moist eyes without tears are the worst kind of crying. It happens when your heart is crushing under the heavy weight of guilt that you feel you are not even allowed to shed a tear for it. But at the same time, the sadness and sweet memories mix like hot and cold surface that the combined emotion forces the waterworks out of the body through the throat.

Abdus flicked her head softly and said, "It is good to look at your past but don't dwell on it too long. The things which are gone will not the comeback but if you stare at it too long, it will expose your wound bit by bit."

Abeedah relaxed in his arms and let go all her thoughts and memories which was keeping him from Abdus. It was their second honeymoon technically. She wanted it to be about them only.

After two and a half hours of drive, they reached Bisrakh. It is a small village in Utter Pradesh which was the birth place of Ravana. While every part of the country was burning of the effigy of Ravana marking his killing by Rama, This village worshipped him for his devotion to Lord Shiva and is one of most intelligent and mighty king of Lanka.

"Sir, we have reached Bisrakh, now where you want to go." The driver asked.

Abdus stepped out of the car, looked at the sun, opened the compass his cell phone, and stared it for ten seconds. Stepped back into the vehicle and said told him to take them to the northeast while closing the door behind him. Abeedah and driver looked at him as if they were saying, "What are you talking about?"

Abdus realized these days people are not much fond of using compass for directions, so he started instructing him with the directions. After half an hour they were about to reach the spot but got stuck in the uneven, muddy road. The place was bustling with people.

Abdus said,"Last time when I was here I hardly saw any people."

"Time has changed Abdus." Abeedah replied.

"But again I am saying you don't get your hopes up. It was just a barren land. The only thing you will see around is abundant land and a reasonable sized Shiv Ling. I think—"As he spilled the last word, he saw a massive temple which had 42 feet tall Shiv Ling which was visible from a distance.

"Oh really! A reasonable sized Shiv Ling on the abandoned land?" Abeedah teased him.

"Oh, sir you wanted to visit the Ravana temple. You should have told me I would have taken you here directly. It is a very famous temple. But I don't understand why they build such huge temple in the name of Ravana and why these people worship him, wasn't he a demon?" The driver asked.

"This is his birthplace and he was not just a demon but the biggest devotee of Lord Shiva and a sagacious person. One mistake cannot define a person." Abdus said in resentment.

Abeedah understood though he was saying this entire thing about Ravana. He was also relating himself to his condition. To make him feel better continued to his statement. "Also he was a great scholar and had ten heads which represented six shastras and four Vedas. His paramount ambition was to overpower and dominate the Gods."

Abdus looked at Abeedah to show how proud he was of her knowledge but also to stop her from talking.

"Okay, sir I will wait here." The driver said.

They stepped out of the car and went inside the temple. The whole place built newly. Abdus found it very hard to find the spot he was looking for. Everyone around him could see his agitation.

"Who are you?" voice made Abeedah turn and found herself facing a savage man, who was looking at them from stairs. Abdus saw Abeedah talking to him and rushed to her side. He recognized the man as Aghori, an ascetic Shaiva sadhu known to engage in post-mortem rituals.

The Aghori had cremated ashes rubbed all over his body. His eyes and that sandalwood paste all over his forehead, the long dreadlocks up to his ankles and weird tiger skin skirt. The look on his face was terrifying. Abeedah was so frightened with his whole demeanor that she couldn't even dare to look at him straight to his face.

Pushing her behind him, Abdus started talking to the Aghori, "What are you looking for?"

He asked again to Abdus, "Who are you? What are you looking for?"

"What do you mean?" Abdus asked.

"I have devoted my life to Mahakaal, and I know when he is here. I can sense a part of Mahakaal in you."

"This is absurd. You are talking nonsense." Abdus said trying to dodge his questions.

"Before this temple, our ancestors prayed to the Shiv Ling which is a little far away surrounded by bushes. When you reach the place where sunshine does not fall on the ground, there stands the Linga you are looking for." Aghori said like he was giving a generalized statement but the statement made sense only to Abdus. Aghori was talking about the Shiv Ling which Abdus was looking for. Abdus took Abeedah's hand and as instructed by the Aghori, they started marching in search of the Shiv Ling.

After walking under the burning sun, at a distance, they saw a small cave-like structure which was more of bushes than rocks. Abdus started walking towards it and saw the Shiv Ling resting under the shed of the Cave. It looked like the bushes were giving him the shed to rest. He pulled off a sturdy branch from the nearby tree and started digging beneath the Ling.

"Abdus, what the hell are you doing? I'm pretty sure you shouldn't vandalise a temple. Again. Even though there is nothing worth vandalizing." She looked around in alarm.

Abdus looked around and replied with a straight face, "Wow Abeedah, there are so many people around who are going to film us and start burning places. How did I miss that?"

"Yeah, no need to sass me. I can't believe after all the drama you brought me here and you are just sitting there digging dirt. What is the part of your past? The soil?" She was a little agitated after her encounter with Aghori and Abdus who was not telling her anything.

Abdus imitated a horrible high pitched female voice and replied animatedly as he kept digging, "Oh Abdus, you don't tell me anything. Oh Abdus, I want to see your past. Oh, Abdus, you are just digging dirt."

This earned him a slap on the back of his head. Abdus just chuckled and then replied continued in a normal voice, "Abeedah, have patience."

After digging couple of feet, he saw a shiny metal. Abeedah unaware of the situation and intentions of Abdus kept silence and sat beside him, figuring out what he was up to by herself. He dug it few more inches and pulled off a huge sword from the muddy ground.

It was huge, bigger than any sword she has seen in movies. The sword was though covered in mud but the blood stains were visible through it. The blade was still shiny, rust free and gems on the hilt still looked brand new, which was very strange because it was buried in the ground for many centuries. For the first time, Abeedah saw Abdus as a warrior that he was, the huge sword in his hand fit him naturally. But she could also see the guilt and fear in his eyes while holding it.

Abdus was a man of words, and so was Abeedah. They both knew the suitable words to say in the right situations. Abeedah knew this is the correct time to repeat back his words. She said, "It's good to look at your past but don't dwell at it too long. The things which are gone will not come back but if you stare at it for too long, it will expose your wound bit by bit."

Abdus sigh and chuckled softly, "Touché. Do you have something to clean it with?"

She took a scarf out of her bag and handed it to him. He walked to a nearby stone, sat on it and started cleaning the sword. Abeedah sat next to him and looked at him. At looked over at Abeedah and the sight of her raised eyebrows he started talking.

"Do you want to know what I see in my nightmares? Whom do I fight?" He kept cleaning the sword, and now Abeedah was able to see the dried blood on the blade, clearly. A gasp escaped her. She tried to scratch away the dried blood hoping it to be mud or something but the blood was matted so thick, it didn't make a difference. It seemed that the metal has soaked up an immense amount of blood.

He continued, guilt and sadness marring his beautiful face, "This is what I dream of. With this weapon in my hand, I see my body kill hundreds of men, under the influence of the power that I asked from Mahakal. I see the horrors done by me because of a decision I made in my stupidity, in anger that changed everything. I fight that person because I never want to be him again. I have the blood of hundreds of lives on my hand and it does't matter how much time passes by, the guilt will never diminish. Though time has passed, and I have been less consumed by the guilt, but it is always in the back of my mind. At least once a day, it comes back to me. "

She was shocked to hear this, unable to find words to say to him.

Abdus looked at her and smiled self depreciatingly, "Usually you don't shut up, and now you don't have anything to say?"

She swatted his arm and asked, "What about this sword? Why did you hide this here, in the middle of nowhere?"

"When I asked Mahakal for his power, he also gave me this sword and told me to return this to his original owner after I was done with it, that in any circumstance I was not to keep it. This sword belonged to Ravana. And, well he was dead, and I didn't know how to return it to him. So I prayed to Shiva, but he didn't appear. I guess he was also very disappointed in me. Anyway, I remembered this as Ravana's birthplace, so I decided that this would be the best way to return it to him."

Abeedah couldn't move her eyes from the gleaming sword, "Why do you think Mahakal told you not to keep it? How would you return it to Ravana when he was already dead?"

Abdus hesitated before replying, "I have thought about it. What I think, after that massacre is that this sword seeks blood. And it couldn't be controlled."

She finally tore her eyes from the sword and looked at him bewildered, "We are not taking this with us, right?"

He laughed at her expression, "No, of course not. You wanted a peek into my past, Abeedah. This is the only piece of my past that I have, although it's ugly. The most shameful and horrific thing I have ever done apart from targeting that unborn child."

He stood up after dusting his pants from the dust and wrapped the sword with the piece of cloth Abeedah gave to him. He placed it on the ground beneath the Shiv Ling and covered it with mud, as he did before. He looked around and said, "It will be with its owner as instructed."

He looked at the clay pot on the side which was filled with water for the travelers passing by. He removed his shoes and lifted the pot and poured the water on the Shiv Ling. His eyes closed, raised his right leg and slowly placing the feet near left leg's knee. The peace in his face after facing his greatest fear and after showing that fear to his love was like the grace of the Sun after a long cold winter night.

For the first time, Abeedah saw him worshiping. No matter how much denial he was in or will be, he could never let himself not to bow down to his patron God, Shiva, who had a different future planned for him, which was beyond his imagination.

Gods and their words have always been a mystery. Every single word coming from them had a hidden meaning, which will only be revealed when the time is right. Lord Shiva also used his words to indicate a future, which no one could expect, which no one can imagine. A plan which will explain all the reasons behind many things that happened in the past, because one always get what they want from the bottom of their heart, climbing at the peak of their dedication towards it but only when the time is right. Everything around us is like dominos.

With this sword, the only barrier that was keeping Abdus and Abeedah to be one was dropped. Abdus never imagined that the part of his life, which he considered so ugly to reveal to Abeedah, could turn out to be a reason to bring them closer. To make them stand united to walk on the path that was waiting for them. For the first time in life after the curse, Abdus was at peace with his past and was living in the present where he could see a future for himself but not alone.

Abdus was no more afraid of himself or what he may turn to be. He was a better person and he knew now he was strong enough, that he cannot turn to be the person that he was ashamed of. Happiness, true happiness, is an inner quality. It is a state of mind. If your mind is at peace, you are happy.

But even after spending centuries on this planet, he was still unaware of the fact that no matter how strong a person is, past and fear always find their way to haunt. It was just the beginning of his happy days. There will be many more days to come when he faces his past and his sins because Karma never let go, anyone, so easily.

Chapter Fourteen

Archery

One year later....

Today was 4th of July, Abdus's cell phone rang with a loud ringtone to alarm him the date. The alarm was a reminder to him to bring chocolates for Abeedah and prepare himself for her worst mood swings. He knew for the next four days he doesn't have any rooms for his mistakes and carelessness at home. Although he was double her size and powerful immortal warrior, he was terrified of her most days but it elevated significantly these few days. He was very peculiar of not leaving the wet towel on the bed or mug stain on the coffee table or kitchen counter. But he treated her like a child being very protective and loving, like a perfect gentleman.

This month he broke the lamp four times, to compensate he decided to stock up double the quantity of chocolates complementing it with her favorite black forest cake, on the way home. But he was surprised to see her smiling face and not to be interrogated with her sullen face. She took the packet from his hand and kept it in the refrigerator.

Even After two days, the cake and chocolates were still untouched. But Abdus was terrified to poke the bear with his question. Abdus never liked the waste of food, especially when it is sweet because of the life he had spent. So he took it out and ate the whole cake alone without leaving any trace of it.

A few days later on a warm Sunday afternoon and the sun was brighter than any other usual day, Abdus received an emergency pick up call from Abeedah. Abeedah was standing on the roadside waiting for Abdus to pick her up after her appointment with a gynecologist. After enduring so much of pain, she was had finally having her share of happiness. The harsh truth of Abdus made her fall in love with him even more. It also helped her in realizing that this world has its other side of meaning as well, the side which is beyond the understanding of a human and his belief. An ocean of mystical secrets has been hidden inside the womb of this earth.

But today, she was happy. She had a distinguishable glow on her face and had never been this eager to see her grey sedan. Her eyes were in search of Abdus, and she was continually looking at her wristwatch repeatedly.

She heard a voice from his back. "Mumbai's traffic and rain is unpredictable, I have heard!"

She turned around and saw an old man trying to talk to her. He had grey hair, kind hazel eyes, well-trimmed beard and little wrinkled skin. She smiled and nodded back. She again turned around to look for Abdus.

"Anyways, congratulations!" said the old man.

She got surprised and curious. "I'm sorry, but what you are congratulating me for?" she asked.

"For your child." he replied with a smile.

Her face turned pale. "How— how did you know?" she asked in a stammering voice.

He pushed up his oval bipolar glass above his nose and replied "The glow on your face is motherly. Although, he will not be a usual child…"

"'What? How do you know that? Who are you?" she asked.

"You shouldn't be out alone. All I can say is neither you nor your child is safe," he warned her.

Abeedah heard a honk behind her and turned to look Abdus waiting for her at the curb.

She turned back and the man was gone. She looked around and shouted, "Wait! Who are you? Wait!"

She heard Abdus calling her. "Are you trying to ignore me?"

She got into the car and shut the door hard. She was breathing heavily. He had felt her agitation on the way to the car's door.

"What happened? Are you okay? Why your face is so pale?"

Another car honked behind them warning them to move along. Abdus started the car and eased on the road, asked her mischievously, "Saw a ghost or what? But after marrying me, you shouldn't feel scared of such things!"

He expected her to laugh but when he turned to look at her, he understood the gravity of situation from Abeedah's stunned face. He asked her to take a deep breath and calm herself down. After she got control on her nerves, she said, "I met an old man who warned me that our baby and I are in danger."

"Baby? Are you pregnant?" He asked as his face lit up. He parked the car sideways; he didn't trust himself as his heart was thudding against his chest upon such happy news.

The very next moment she realized that she had spoiled the surprise of this news. Abdus couldn't comprehend how to react to such unbelievable news. He never thought that he would become a father in his life again. Not after Nituna.

"But that man, what he sa—" she said.

"Forget him," he interrupted. "Might be some lunatic roaming on the road. Everyone who could have harmed our child are all dead. Don't worry. Are you sure?"

"Yes, I'm sure. I just confirmed it with the doctor," She beamed overjoyed with his infectious happiness evident on his face.

"We need to celebrate this news! You are giving me that which I am not destined to. I still wonder how this happening is. But, it is happening. I love you more than my life Abeedah." He took her face in his hands and kissed her softly but with no less passion.

This day was the happiest one in their life, but Abeedah was having enormous difficulty ignoring the old man's words.

For the purpose of celebrating, Abdus took her out in one of their favorite restaurant in Bandra for dinner. It was a 10th-floor open roof restaurant. He, being a nature lover, loved to watch the horizon of city lights and the natural darkness of the night. He gifted Abeedah a small wrapped box. It had a necklace with a tiny broken piece of purple gem. She smiled and complimented, "This is beautiful."

"Abeedah it's a broken gem. Unlike any other gem, it has some unusual powers to protect you. I know you are worried about our child, but I am worried about both of you. This gem is so powerful that even its broken piece has the power of resurrection. Never take it off, ever, come what may. Promise me."

"I promise. But from where did you get this stone?" she asked curiously.

"I was born with this on my forehead. But when I pleaded for apology against my sin, Vasudev asked my gem as a punishment. While removing it from my forehead, a small piece of it was broken, and since then I have kept it with me. Today, I want you to wear it because I can't afford to lose you and our child." He said.

After their dinner they went for a romantic walk on the shore of the beach holding hands. At night, the sea usually appears dreamy under the twinkling stars. It has a rhythmic pulse in its waves which is incomparable to any other part of nature. It echoes its own sound and creates its own symphony. The breathless waves were waiting for the full tide, and their whispering was mesmerizing. They felt like they were walking on a carpet of candy floss.

It was soothing to their senses. The golden sand swept around in its own curve forming a tower of dunes. The neon-blue sky made its way in a silvery appearance.

Abeedah couldn't help but compare Abdus with the dreamy sea. He had lived for five thousand years with an unknown identity. He was all alone and suffered in silence yet he smiles just like those shaky waves controlling its mighty power.

Abdus had been and is now an equal part of this new world. He had managed to inculcate this modern culture just like a wave gets itself absorbed by touching the sands of the beach.

Admiring his calmness and happiness, she felt that her life purpose is now served. She was feeling alive than usual and was very excited for the new phase. All her worries had bowed down and all she was left with was to live in that moment. Neither the future nor her past haunted her at that time. She could feel the waves touching her, and when it went back to the sea, her feet were covered with a cool breeze. Indeed life has its own way to decide what and when to give to someone.

A few days later Abdus received a call from National Field Archery Association, India.

"Hello, Mr. Samad. This is Swastik Shankar this side calling on behalf of National Field Archery Association India. Is this good time to talk?"

"Yes, of course!"

Unaware of the organization he quickly checked it on his laptop and googled "National Field Archery Association." He was handling the call simultaneously. He also realized that it is not an ordinary call for sure.

"Mr. Samad are you there?"

"Yes! Yes! I am here. Please, what can I do for you?"

After attending the call, he went into the kitchen where Abeedah was cooking dinner. He hugged her from behind and said, "Darling, I just received a call from National Field Archery Association. They have invited me to attend a meeting to discuss Manik."

Abeedah halted from her kitchen work and asked by raising her eyebrows. "Discuss what?"

"They want Manik to represent India in commonwealth Game 2010!"

"Really? You are not kidding, right?

"They want me and Manik to attend a meeting with the council where he will be performing for the selection trial."

She turned around and hugged him tightly, "Oh my God! This is a huge deal Abdus! I am so happy for you and Manik."

Next day early morning Abdus got ready for the big day. As he walked by the door, he stopped and went back to Abeedah asking her to bring curd and sugar.

Abeedah asked." What you want curd and sugar for?"

He explained to her how her loving mother, Kripi twin sister of Kripacharya always made him eat a spoon of curd and sugar every day before leaving home, it was considered as a spoon of good luck charm. Today was the big day for him in this new life. He missed his mother and her tender touch. Abeedah brought a bowl of curd and sugar to give him the same good luck charm as his mother. With the sweet and sour taste of curd in his mouth, he left home.

On the way to the parking, he called Rajat to inform Manik that he will be there to pick him up in sharp forty minutes. He was very particular about timing. It was unexpected for a man who had all the time in the world to give such importance to it. After sharp forty minutes, he reached Manik's home where he was waiting for him on the street with his big bag on the shoulder.

Manik has been responding to his medicines and treatments aggressively. It was a surprise for his father to see such progress in his health and attitude. He had little sprinkles of hair growing on his head, and his lethargic face was transferred to a conviction. Though there was still a slight gauntness to his face, the darkness near his eyes which indicated his feeble health was now purged from his skin color popping up the enlivened. They continued the journey after greeting each other.

Chapter fifteen

The oath of Panchali

Before entering the academy hall, Manik stopped at the doorstep and touched Abdus's feet for his blessings. Abdus heartfelt with the warmth and respect his action. He always adored Manik for his politeness. At that moment he saw his unborn child's reflection on him. He held Manik's hand which was shivering and sweaty, to give the confidence he needs.

Before the selection trial, the Chairman started his motivational speech, "Welcome participants. Delhi will be a host to XIX Commonwealth Games 2010 next October with a record-equaling 17 disciplines confirmed for competition. Among the 17 is archery, one of the first-born sporting events known to our humankind.

As per the records, archery event was held for once in 1982 in Brisbane Games. This time, it will be for the second time in the history. Around 125 athletes from 24 countries have registered to participate in the Commonwealth Games New Delhi 2010. The Delhi archery competition will take place at the Yamuna Sports Complex from 4-10 October 2010 with some of the best archers in the world.

The Delhi 2010 Games will see competition in both recurve archery and compound bow sections. There will be eight gold, eight silvers and eight bronze medals on offer. Championships will be held in the team, and individual events of men's and women's recurve and compound sections. The finals are expected to be played at the famous lawns of India Gate! I wish good luck to all the participants!"

One by one all the participants started performing in their own modern techniques. Everyone had their own style. They had this attitude of a warrior in their face while shooting which reminded Abdus of his learning days where he used to learn archery in the open environment under the sky supported by nature.

Abdus remembers the little jealousy he felt when his father called Arjun his best student. He also recalled how Pandavas made him feel undermined and weak, especially Arjun. At this time Duryodhana was the one who considered him a true friend and not the son of their Guru. Though Duryodhana followed unrighteous path many times in his life, he had always been a good friend to him. He always regretted the moment where he would have changed the climax of the war if he could have little better in convincing Duryodhana to make peace with Pandavas. He recalled his last conversation with Duryodhana.

After the death of Dushasana in the hand of Bhima and Draupadi washing her long perfect black hair with his blood, her hand and her hair soaked in red. It was a sight nobody could take off their mind from the scene who ever witnessed. Her oath and her loose hair have craved for Dushasana's blood for many years. She looked no less than Goddess Kali at the moment. But this was just the begging, Ashwatthama knew the Pandavas would not stop at any cost and Vasudev at their side will make it inevitable.

Ashwatthama went to the Duryodhana room, while passing through the hallways of the palace with Gothic style architecture. The entrance was shining like a soothing fire from the reflection of the torch on the golden wall art, and the reflection from multicolored gens made various patterns on the floor. Everything reflects the golden rays of the sun. It seems bright enough, in comparison to the mortal kingdom. The carpet was soft like velvet.

Ashwatthama had many things going on his head, but the only solution he found out was a peace treaty between Kauravas and Pandavas. This was the only way of keeping both the clans safe. He knew Vasudev would be onboard with this decision coming from Duryodhana's mouth. Wrangling up with every possible way to convince Duryodhana, he reached his chamber where he found him looking out of his unframed window and glazing the far barren land which looked like his life, if he lost the war, Empty. He turned towards the door after hearing the door knocking. He saw his childhood friend Ashwatthama standing at the door.

"Come on in, my friend. You don't need my permission to enter my chamber." Duryodhana said.

"I am here to pay my condolences for Dushasana's death. He was your beloved brother." Ashwatthama said.

"When you enter a war one should be prepared for all kind of situations except for losing it.

I am happy that I still have friends like you and Karna on my side. You two are enough for me to win the war." Duryodhana said.

Ashwatthama took a deep breath, with the white cloth wrapped around his wrist flowing through his shoulders and white silk dhoti, which he wore every night after the fight to pay condolences to all the lives that were lost in the battle from both the side, he paced around and said "There is four kind of friends, the first kind of a friend is a natural friend, without any reason. Second kind is one who becomes a friend by chance. The third kind is one who makes a friend by purchasing friendship, and fourth is one who on being influenced by the power of a person, wants to be the friend of such personality."

He continued, "Since you are born in the same family you can be natural friends, and you could also have a truce with them and save the remaining Kuru clan."Ashwatthama was convinced that the Pandavas would agree to the truce.

Duryodhana heard and took a long pause as if he was considering Ashwatthama's suggestion but concluded that it was not possible. He said "After seeing how Dushasana was killed, it will be an insult to Karna, who is capable of killing Arjuna, to make a truce. So there is no question of friendship with Pandavas."

It made Ashwatthama sad to see his dear friend had lost the qualification to befriend anyone. He was looking to kill the very people Ashwatthama was asking him to befriend. Also, he never genuinely liked Karna, he believed that he was friends with Duryodhana for his own benefits, but he always respected his skills and high merits. He had forgotten the crime he had committed he merely remembered the death of Dushasana at the hands of Bhima, one of the Pandavas.

Ashwatthama surrendered his words and went back to his chamber, without making much effort to convince his friend, which would have changed the conclusion of the war and could have the cause of his own life too.

But what happened brought him here, where he is standing in his life with her beloved wife Abeedah on his side, bearing his child and Manik, the best student he had.

Manik's voice brought him back from his nostalgia, "Sir! Sir! It's my turn now."

It was now Manik's turn. His hands were shaking, and his palm was sweating. His nervousness was evident to everyone who was watching him. Abdus patted his back and said, "You can do this son. Trust me."

A thin, short girl, standing next to him, tried to console Manik after noticing his nervousness. "Everyone here is nervous. The first rule of any competition is not to show your flaws, especially to your competitors. Either you will win or lose, there is no third alternative. So just do it and forget everything for a moment. Give your best!"

He looked at Abdus, and his support gave him a little confidence. The first event was to shoot 2 *60 meters for ranking. Manik couldn't pull the target but scored 640. He got qualified for the second game which was one to one round robin match.

After going through numerous rounds of competition, only ten of them were selected for the final round, and Manik was one of them. Though he lacked confidence use of traditional techniques impressed the judges.

The news was intimated to Abdus on the call. Next day he shared this news with Manik and his father, Rajat. Rajat was dumbstruck with joy. It was his lifetime achievement, and it was apparently visible on his face. He had waited for this time for years. He hugged Manik just like a new mother hugs her newborn as soon as she holds her baby for the first time. Rajat in his teary eyes showed his gratitude for Abdus. Gratitude for trusting his son when nobody did. Joy is contagious and his cheerfulness quickly spread into the eyes of Abdus and Manik.

"Start packing! I will make all the necessary arrangements." Rajat said delightfully.

"But first we need to practice," said Manik.

Being fifteen year old, Manik had achieved his adolescence quiet early. Abdus was highly impressed with his sense of logic and sincerity. A relationship between coach and a student was gradually transforming into a deep-rooted bond, growing stronger day by day. Without communicating much, they got along very smoothly. They understood each other's behavior which was quite overwhelming for both of them.

Abdus asked Manik to carry his compound bow and arrows.

"Sir, where are we going? No practice today?"

"Today we are going to practice in the real world and not inside those four walls."

"Is it safe?"

"In our days, we never had any fancy bows or a practice room. We used to practice on nature's lap." Abdus replied.

Abdus drove his car, and they stopped at a place which was surrounded by nature. No market, no restaurants, not even a residency. It was a calm place best suited for meditation. They stood on the cliff from where they could see a rupture of white sand, a gash of wind- haunted cliffs and a wide slash of the bay.

The horizon was a thin layer where the covering of sky and the plane of sea met in the form of cracks in the cloud. The breeze was very powerful to push them back as if marking its territory forcefully. Abdus took a deep breath of the fresh breeze "It has been said that Paradise is where seagull is flying beneath your feet."

He bent down and took the soil in his hand. "Archery is not a game. It's a warrior's life. A true archer is the one who feels and respects the elements of nature. Learn to respect the sky because they will help you with direction. Respect the wind as they stimulate the speed. When you respect the sun, he helps in fostering your concentration and energy. Respect this soil. It will help you in maintaining your stability. Most importantly, when you respect and listen to your conscious, it will help you in aiming your target.

Respect these elements of nature, and they will guide your wit. But, they will never pave the path for you because that is your goal. Manik, this world is full of distractions and diversions. There are many evil elements including some humans who will try to divert your attention towards your doom. So what we can do? The more you will connect with nature, the less will be the impression of this world upon you. Always remember this."

Manik was listening very seriously as if he was meditating. He closed his eyes as if trying to connect his senses with nature. Suddenly he opened his squinting eyes and said, "Nothing is happening, I don't hear anything, I don't feel anything. What am I exactly looking for?" He was confused.

"We all are looking for something. We don't know that unknown, and this is our life's purpose to know the unknown. Breathe. Just calm yourself. When you connect with your subconscious mind, you will be automatically connected sync with nature. All you have to do is to minimize your worldly thoughts and try to listen to the musings of nature."

Manik admired Abdus a lot, but today Manik felt as if long-awaited thirst had been quenched. Abdus was now not only his coach but a father figure.

Manik took a deep breath and closed his eyes. Gradually he bent his one knee and touched the earth. He could feel the movement of molecules in his palm and could sense the echo and feel of the wind and sunlight. He was then blessed by the rising sun. At that moment, it appeared that Manik was an exceptional soul and the wind was crowning its pride.

Abdus's guidance and nature's support gave him enough strength of being a warrior. He stood upright with a straight back and dipped chest, placed his feet firmly, shoulder - width apart pointed towards a tree at a distance. He knocked the arrow using his three fingers. He raised the bow in a semicircle. It was cutting the edges of the wind. He drew the bow aiming at the center of the trunk of the tree and released the arrow. It steadily pierced the middle of the chest. He took the second shaft and aimed at the first arrow. It went tearing it apart into three pieces. Abdus felt proud and applauded for his perfect strike. He said, "Bull's eye! Now that you are physically and technically trained to compete, focus on strengthening your mental and moral planes. Desire, engagement, ability and plan ~ these are the ways to achieve your objectives."

"Sir, I think I will win surely!" Manik said proudly by raising his nose in the air.

Abdus chuckled and said, "Have you heard this quote? -'The intoxication with power is worse than drunkenness with liquor and such, for who is drunk with power does not come to his —"

"His senses before he falls" Manik completed the sentence by gazing at the floor.

Abdus was surprised. He asked, "How do you know that?"

With an ironic smile on his face ", I might have heard this from the man who had created this quote, and I know that I am going to win." Abdus chuckled after listening to his words because the man who created this quote was Vidura. They both laughed and headed back towards home.

Chapter Sixteen

Here comes Mrityu

The very next day, they had a flight to Delhi to meet the council. It was difficult for Abdus to leave Abeedah alone. It was for the first time he was leaving her alone since the time they have met. It was even scary because he was aware of the fact that apart from her, their child was also in need of protection. His sleep got interrupted now and then with such thoughts. When sunlight made its way through the glass, and rays fell on her cheeks, she looked no less than a princess. She was glowing in golden and was at peace in her sleep. Her calmness highlighted that she might be enjoying her own world of dreams.

For Abdus, it was more soothing to watch her than to admire the sunrise. He didn't wake her up. He was aware that it would become impossible to leave her once he looked into her innocent, dreamy eyes filled with love for him. So, he took out the 'John Denver - Leaving on a Jet Plane' from his record collection and stuck a post on it saying "Couldn't break your dream! Will be back soon, love" and left to catch the taxi waiting outside.

On his way to the airport, he got a feeling that someone was following him, but whenever he turned around, he couldn't find anyone but the crowd busy with their own set of daily race. He thought that might be his anxiety was taking over his conscious. He saw Rajat and Manik waiting at the airport with their boarding pass. As they left for the terminal, Rajat got emotional and hugged his son a gentle goodbye.

Abdus never saw any dispute between both of them, but he could always feel a gap between the father and the son. Rajat loved Manik with all his heart, but Manik never looked much bothered about his father. His actions and reactions tried to mean as if he always denied the fact that Rajat is his father. On the other hand, Abdus's heart and mind were clogged up in the thoughts of Abeedah. He always kept thinking about her throughout his flight. When they landed, he checked his cell phone which beeped with her message "You can never break my dream because you are one of a kind! Don't worry I will take care of myself and our baby properly. You too take care of yourself and my best wishes to Manik.

Come back soon; we are waiting!" He smiled while reading her message.

By 11 A.M, they entered the venue before the selection trial. The Chairman started his motivational speech. "I sincerely welcome all the participants. Delhi will be hosting XIX Commonwealth Games 2010 next October with 17 disciplines definite for the competition. Among the 17 is the archery, one of the oldest sporting events known to our humankind. The finals are expected to be played at the famous lawns of India Gate! Good luck to all the participants!"

Gradually, the participants performed with their own modern techniques.

Manik was a little nervous but much confident after his session. His hands were steady enough which proved his self belief. A sense of calmness prevailed on his face. All the noise surrounded him and inside him was calm, for the time being. This time, the people around were amazed to see his confidence, and the other participants felt nervous.

Abdus's said last words before his turn, "This is it Manik. Just close your eyes, recall the lesson you had yesterday in the lap of nature and aim it. Don't think that you want to win. Think that you will be the best archer today. Best of luck."

"Right, Sir. I believe in your lessons and blessings. I believe in my learning, and today, I have started believing in myself. Vision is all that matters. I will try my best to portray my vision by my archery to all the people who are watching this. Today, these people, their cheers or their hatred is not distracting me. I can feel a sudden change in myself. All this is because of you. Thank you, thank you for being my coach."

"Now go!" Abdus patted his back proudly.

Manik before picking up his bow he brought both his bands back near the waist, stretched his left wrist with the right hand and right wrist with left making joint cracking sound and then he did the same thing with his fingers. Abdus had seen this stretching back in his past, as Karna used to do the same thing as a gesture of his preparation. Of course, this move might not be very rare, but today he saw Karna in place of Manik. They had the very similar feature and story, which gave him Karna's resemblance.

Here in Mumbai, Abeedah was eagerly waiting for Abdus's call. In excitement, she started walking back and forth in the room when she heard the doorbell ringing. It was Mrs. Harshwardhan. She immediately entered her house with a cheerful face and shouted "Abeedah what are you doing? Switch on the TV!"

"Mrs. Harshwardhan ? What happened? Is everything alright?"

"Abeedah you really ask too many questions! Give me the remote."

Manik was selected for the finals. It was a live coverage, and as soon as they saw Abdus standing with him, Mrs. Harshwardhan and Abeedah both started jumping like a little girls. They both were thrilled. Abeedah gently sat down on her couch and touched her belly. She said, "Do you know baby whom I saw right now on the TV? Your daddy!" It was indeed a wonderful day for Abeedah, Manik, and Abdus.

Today was the day that Manik has eagerly waiting for. It was a day before the final performance of Manik. Abeedah's belly had started showing, and she started feeling the presence of the baby inside her. This time, Abdus asked Abeedah to accompany him to Delhi. All excited, she did her packing and went to handover a spare key of her house to Mrs. Harshwardhan for any unexpected emergencies.

By that time, Abdus went to call the cab, and they left for the airport. It was a rush hour. People were getting back from their work, and they got stuck in traffic. Amidst all these, Abeedah forgot to take her evening medicine. Abdus being very particular about her and their child's health, asked the taxi driver to pull over on the side of a medical store.

"Leave it we are getting late for our flight. It is about to rain Abdus. I can manage…"

"Don't worry I will be quick. I can't take any risk with you and our child." He left her in the taxi and went inside a drugstore. It had started drizzling, but it seemed as if a massive storm was approaching them.

While she watched him crossing the road, she thought to herself that what she could have done that she had Abdus in her life. She was admiring him when she heard a cell phone ringing. It was Mr. Rajat calling Abdus. She picked up the phone.

"Hello! Hello! Abdus?" Rajat said. His voice was tensed.

"Hello, Mr. Rajat. I am Abeedah."

"Abeedah, where is Abdus?" Rajat started panicking.

"He is inside a store. What happened? Is everything all right?" she asked.

"I need to talk to him very urgently. Manik is missing!" he said.

"What? Okay, just hold on!" She immediately stepped outside the taxi, calling Abdus's name. It was a busy street, and due to horning of vehicles along with distance, her voice was barely audible for Abdus. She started walking towards him, and it started raining heavily with all thunder. She looked up towards the sky unpleasantly. As she placed back her eyes towards Abdus, everything around her turned dull. The horns of vehicles had stopped, the voice of the people around had stopped, and everything felt paused. The only thing she could feel was thunder, rain, and cold.

Abeedah could see Abdus, but her throat was chocked. She desperately wanted to call out his name but failed to utter a single word from her mouth. Before she could understand anything that was happening, she saw black smoke coming from her left and right. The smoke tried to cover her vicinity, and there she saw those Reapers again. They didn't have those eyes of a human still Abeedah she could feel them staring at her. Her body turned cold as ice. The speed of her breath increased but turned shallow. She was under the situation of panic, and she could feel some cluster of spark plugging in her abdomen. The only movement which she was able to hear was her breath panting.

Abeedah's body was numb, and she dropped the mobile from her hand. Within few seconds, the Reapers disappeared into thin air and everything was in motion again. But before she could regain her senses, she was standing in the middle of the road. She heard Abdus's voice calling her, "Abeedah!!"

Abdus shouted holding some medicines in one hand and chocolates in the other. He was shocked to see her in the middle of the road. He tried to reach the road trying to stop her, but before he could reach out, a car in speed went hitting Abeedah.

Then everything seemed to slow down like a slow motion scene from a movie. Abdus saw Abeedah falling down and hitting her head and heard her cry of pain. The medicines and chocolates left his hand and he ran towards her. Around them people started gathering to see what happened and the person who hit Abeedah came out to see her. Abdus fell to his knees and took her in his arms.

The guy who hit her also knelt beside them, his voice shaking, "Is she okay? She was just standing in the middle of the road and I couldn't control my car? I'm really sorry."

Abdus was so enraged he pushed the guy so hard who fell away from them, "You filthy bastard, you hurt my Abeedah!"

Turning his attention back to her, he consoled her looking into her eyes, "Abeedah, it's okay. We'll take you to the hospital. You will be fine. Our little baby will be fine, don't you worry. Stay with me? Just stay with me."

She was barely breathing. The pain that once burned like fire had faded away to an icy numbness as soon as Abdus took her in his arms. Her vision slowly turned black and she could only hear her own heartbeat. With all her effort, she wanted to move her hand and wipe Abdus's shedding tears, but her dying body didn't allow her to do so. She wanted to tell Abdus how much she loves him but her voice was chocked from the trauma. Still, her dying eyes conveyed him her massages.

Abeedah could see all her happy moments of her life in front of her eyes. Her laugh echoed and all she could see was Abdus's face. Abdus saw his hand was all covered in her blood. An agonizing scream left his heart. And with the slow breath of Abeedah, Abdus's world started falling like a castle of cards.

He couldn't believe his eyes and his senses. He denied her death. It can't be. She is breathing albeit slowly. Abdus lifted her in her arms and ran back to the car, slid in with cradling her body and barked the cab driver to go to nearest hospital.

No, Abeedah cannot die. He was finally happy and he wouldn't let anyone take anything from him again, certainly not Abeedah and his child. He will fight anyone and everyone to make sure that Abeedah will be safe.

He yelled at the taxi driver to drive faster or he will wring his neck. Finally with a screech the cab stopped in front of the hospital, Abdus lifted Abeedah and ran towards the ER, yelling for doctors to help his wife. Doctors ran to him and asked him to lay her on a stretcher and took her to the emergency room, asking Abdus to stay outside and wait.

Abdus sat outside with blood on his hands and clothes for who knows how long. He always doubted his happiness that how long it will last but the moment he heard the good news, he was settling in it. They had started believing that this is their life now, he had paid his debt, and it was now his turn to be happy and live a normal life. But it was inevitable that he was wrong, that his debt has not been paid yet.

Abdus was numb to his feet, and his heart felt as if someone is crushing it from inside making it difficult to beat and breathe. Even after his curse and loneliness, he was adamant to live because it was a physical wound which he learned to bear but an emotional wound is something a person will never get used to. He was still grieving for his father's death and now this.

No, it can't be. He won't let anything happen to Abeedah and their child. It just cannot happen. She will be fine, a little banged up but fine. Abdus was shaking head to toe, his body rocking back and forth. Outside the rain and thunder grew stronger as if they were grieving for him. Tears make it easy to release the sadness, but when one has been through many worse situations, it becomes difficult for them even to cry when they want. Even tears were playing tricks with Abdus.

After a long time, one doctor came to Abdus and spoke softly, "Mr. Abdus? Hello, I'm Doctor Batra and I'm treating your wife. Her injuries were severe and there was too much bleeding. Somehow miraculously Abeedah is alive but she is at very critical stage. We cannot say for sure if we can save her but we are trying our best. She has been transferred to ICU."

"And the baby?" He asked hopefully.

"I'm really sorry Abdus, we couldn't save your baby." She replied sadly, making Abdus's heart skip a beat.

"Can I see her? Abdus choked.

"Yes, you can." She replies with sympathy and led Abdus through a series of corridors and into the Intensive Care Unit.

He looked at her hooked to various machines and bandaged face and body. She looked frail and there was a sickly sheen to her face. He sat beside her and carefully took her hands in his, whispering everything and nothing, asking her to stay, ordering her to not leave him alone and begging her to come back to him. Her hands were cold and her heartbeat very faint.

He randomly started saying everything that made her smile or laughs. He said, "When will you realise that I am a great ca—." He couldn't complete the sentence as Abdus knew the he will not see the same reaction on her face he is expecting.

He was enduring all his physical pain, but the pain of losing a loved one is unbearable. He was bargaining with Vasudev in his head, "If I am supposed to bear pain always. I accept the physical pain again but free me from this pain. Save her, I beg of you, she is innocent."

Afterwards, a ward boy entered the ICU to check on things. As he was checking her reading, suddenly the air in the room shifted and slowed down but not for Abdus. The ward boy stood still and the beeping sound coming from Abeedah's ECG machine also slowed.

Suddenly, he saw a gentleman in a black suit standing at the foot of Abeedah's bed. He was a middle aged man with balding head and a stern face and upturned nose. He mouth was set in a grim line and he had an aura of ownership and arrogance around him like he owns the world. He walked to him indicating he knew Abdus very well, not the only acquaintance. The stranger came to him and stared for a while from top to bottom with calculative gleam in his eyes admiring his changed personality.

"Who are you? What are you?" Abdus shouted.

With a deep sigh, he sat beside him bending his right knee. "A cut or a bruise is nothing in front of emotional pain. A person who faces it knows it how it is. Sometimes, our pain dwells at the back of our mind like a pulse. Other times, it pushes itself forward demanding acute attention. It cuts your heart and mind in half and stings your breath every moment." he said wisely.

"Who are you? Do you know me?" Abdus asked, his anger barely concealed.

"Yes, I know you, O great Ashwatthama. In fact, I know you very well. I have seen your beginning, and defiantly will see your end too." He continued after a pause, "I am the one who can bring your collapsed world to life!" he replied proudly.

"What do you mean? How do you know my name?" Abdus was shocked to hear his real name from a strange man's mouth.

Without saying anything, he pulled his sleeves, and he touched Abeedah's neck gently.

"Hey, don't touch her!" Abdus warned the man but he simply ignored and removed his hand and adjusted his cufflinks. Abdus watched everything in awe.

With that, Abeedah started breathing better and in slowed time he saw her heartbeat registering faster on the ECG.

Abdus couldn't believe what he saw. He asked again, "Who are you? What did you do to her? Abeedah? Abeedah, are you alright?" He was confused what was happening in front of him.

"My name is Mrityu, son of Kali. I did not bring her back to life. It was your broken stone! I just gave it enough power to resurrect her."

"And my child?" he asked with hope in his eyes.

"The stone cannot bring your child back," he replied.

"But you can! You are Mrityu!" Abdus begged.

"Yes. I can. It's my duty to carry away a soul from the dead but granting one back? It isn't my thing. Karma will bite you back when you least expect her. It is your karma, Ashwatthama. The day you intended to murder an unborn in a mother's womb, you were under the debt of karma and karma spares no one. Not even me!" He said politely.

"Then why are you saving her? What is the reason behind such pity?"

Mrityu's eyes widened in dramatic flair, "Oh no! The day I start feeling pity, I won't be able to do my job. This is the reason I don't have a heart. By granting you this favor, you are under my debt now, and when the day will come, I will seek your help, and you won't be able to deny it. Although she wasn't supposed to die now, she has a fate of her own."

Abeedah's little whimper stole Abdus's attention as he turned towards her. Her eyes were moving behind her eyelids, and some color had returned to her face. Abdus turned back to look at Mrityu, but he vanished. Time returned to its normal pace and the ward boy moved as if not a single second has passed. He seemed at surprise how suddenly the patient looked better where one moment before she was on verge of collapsing. He ran out of the room to call a doctor.

Abdus didn't bother to pay too much of attention to that and focused on his lover. Abeedah's breathing became strong and she finally responded to his calls. As she opened her eyes, he regained his own breath. He ran his hand through her hair and kissed her sweet and gentle face.

"Abeedah, are you okay? Can you understand me?" Abdus asked softly.

She nodded slowly, still in pain. Her head was pounding as if she had banged her head on wall to hard.

"Never do this to me, again!" He said with tears in his eyes.

As she gained her consciousness, she remembered her accident, the car hitting her. She touched her belly. She could feel her empty womb. In a state of shock and confusion, she asked, her voice dry and croaked, "My baby? What happened to my baby?"

Abdus looked at her with tears streaming down his cheeks, "We couldn't save it."

She recalled the moment where she had seen those Reapers. She remembered her accident, and she understood that she had lost her unborn child. She screamed in agony. Abdus wrapped his arms around her while she cried for her lost child.

The doctors came to check up on her miraculous recovery and moved her to their private room. After crying for hours, she drifted to sleep in his arms as they both mourned for their lost baby.

Finally placing her on bed, Abdus turned to sit on the chair, keeping an eye on her.

What Abdus didn't see, was an unusually large eagle wrapped on old dirty white bandages like Egyptian Mummies perched on the tree outside their window, witnessing the whole scenario. It looked like a pet bird. It had a golden ring like thing in one of its toe which had a reflection of a yellow diamond in the sunlight. It flew away, leaving Abdus mourn his lost child.

Chapter Seventeen

Dream on, little broomstick cowboy,

THREE YEARS LATER.

WAIT' a four - letter word. It sounds quite simple still it's difficult when it comes to the practical aspect of life. There is a saying, "Whatever a human craves in his life be it, peace of mind, serenity, the awareness of our subconscious it will be granted but only when he is eligible to receive with a contented heart." But when comes to waiting for the ultimate happiness of your life, you feel suffocated unless that joy comes in your life. In our life, we are, and we will be waiting for something or other throughout. The truth of life is maintaining a balance between reasons and result and reasons simply don't count.

For Abdus, a person who has been waiting for 5000 years, patience wouldn't use word 'golden' for it. A stone near the seashore waiting for the sea to touch it gently is an ideal waiting. It's serene and peaceful. Neither the rock is in hurry nor the sea. They both meet on their own destined time. Another form of waiting hits your gut directly. Wait leads to palpitation, a sense of anxiety which pushes you to rub your hands together tightly. Abdus was experiencing this kind of wait.

His sweat was dark which was marking its way towards Abdus's shirt, turning it from a sky blue toward navy blue. His heart was pounding hard as if it will sink in the next moment. His stomach was filled with butterflies of nervousness as he saw the doctors coming out of the operation theatre. It was that kind of wait for him.

"The baby's head is stuck, she is tired. She wants you inside with her. Try to calm her otherwise, we will have serious complications in the delivery." one of the Doctor said to Abdus.

Hearing doctor's words Abdus got tensed, as he knew the reason behind losing his first child and at this point of time he was ready to pay any cost just to get an opportunity to go back to his past and change the awful sin he committed, because this time he was afraid for Abeedah. He knew she won't be able to handle if anything happened to their child again.

He prayed from his heart to Lord Shiva for the protection of his child and his wife and stood up from the iron chair. For few seconds his legs were stuck to the ground and heart pounded slowly and heavily. He could heart every frightened warm breath on his upper lips. He was still dwelling on his past. But today was the biggest moment of his eternal life, and there was no room for his nervousness.

He started walking through the hallway. It was while the color of the walls gave him drowsiness, the flickering of the lights on the roof was making things harder for him, but his legs speeded up, and he rushed into the operation theatre and saw Abeedah lying on a clean sheet crying in pain. He held her hand and said, "I know it's hard. It's hard for me too because I can't see you in such a pain. It's unbearable for me. But Abeedah for last three years, every single day we have been waiting for this moment. I wish I could have endured your pain, but I am here with you. I won't let you give up. Please do it, do it for me, for us? For our child!

In such intense moment, under immense pain and heavy breathing Abeedah said," Can I ask you one thing Abdus?"

"Yes of course anything." He said as if he will easily pull off his guts bare hands if she asked for it.

"Please promise me, after we go back to home you will stop watching Bollywood movies. You sound more like Shah Rukh Khan and less like my husband" She screamed as her pain increased. It's been ten hours since she started feeling the contractions. Some she barely noticed while others erupted like a volcano. Even in her pain, she made herself and Abdus laugh.

Abeedah pulled all her strength and started pushing. Her labor pain got intense. She was facing an ultimate pain of her life. Her stomach tightened. She heard her own scream without being aware of making it, breathing heavily waiting for the agony to subdue. Finally, after struggling with that unbearable pain for forty minutes, she felt the baby crowning, the hot stretching of flesh and held her breath. Without any further effort, the baby slid into the hands of the doctor. It was a boy for Abdus and Abeedah.

When she held him in her arms, Abdus placed his hand beneath his head. It was the purest thing they have ever seen. Abdus looked into those promising little eyes, and it opened up with all kinds of innocence that exist in this world. His little fingers were trying to hold his father's thumb for his affection. At that moment, he knew he would do anything to protect his child and will always stand before him as firm as a rock.

Unknowingly, this child will be changing their lives. The baby boy started rooting. She brought him close to her heart and sobbed. Those were her tears of joy. She felt the motherhood in her heart, and she knew she was a mother now and will always be until her last breath. With the first tender touch of their child, they experienced a fact that their world has now expanded. After some days, she will forget all her pain as good as formatting her memory. One thing she would always recall is the love she felt for her baby, the extended version of her and Abdus, their pure love.

Abeedah never had an experience of what is a mother's love. She never had a loving childhood like a child usually has. She held him to her chest tightly. She looked into his eyes and touched his tiny feet. She said, "I would never let you go, my precious little love! No matter what happens, I would protect you. Even to the point of my death, I promise you, my son."

She looked at Abdus and asked, "What should we call him?"

"We will call him Drona" he replied with affection. He already had decided this name for the baby boy since he knew he was going to be a father.

"Drona!" she repeated and looked at him.

The baby smiled for the first time after hearing his name.

It was Drona's first night at home. He was constantly crying. Something was bothering him. Life outside the womb is quite severe. The air around him feels cold. It was an unknown world to him. Abeedah's womb was his heaven, and he was unable to adjust to this new environment. He screamed in a way as if his voice would shake the pillars of the house. Abeedah was still weak and tired. Her body needed rest, and right now she wanted to sleep to regain her strength. Abdus got up and held Drona on his shoulder. He couldn't believe how tiny babies are and how vulnerable and at the same time they are influential to change someone's life.

He softly patted his back and walked back and forth. Even the soft touch of a warrior's hand was not comforting Drona's delicate bones. Drona was in no mood to settle so easily. He was not willing to stop his scream, in fact, it grew louder and louder. He started kicking Abdus with his tiny toes as if trying to say, "I want my mother, not you!"

Abdus looked at him and said, "You are as stubborn as your grandfather, son. But today, you have to deal with your father." Drona started staring at his father. He was still sobbing. "You know my mother told me that when I was born, I cried like a horse!" he chuckled. He went to his record collection and selected one of his favorite songs and plugged in the gramophone.

He took little Drona in his arms and sat on the rocking chair. "I hope you have the same taste in music as your father. Do you? " He widened his eyes to make Drona understand what he was trying to say.

As the music came out from the gramophone, Abdus sang along, saying those words to his son.

Dream on, little broomstick cowboy,
Of rocket ships and Mars
On sunny days,
And Willie Mays,
And chocolate candy bars
Dream on, little broomstick cowboy,
Dream while you can
Of big green frogs,
And puppy dogs,
And castles in the sand.

Little Drona stopped crying as the first chorus ended and by the end of the coda he slept. His head was lying on his father's chest where he could hear the rhythm of his father's heartbeat. His tiny finger curled making a fist, and he slept peacefully lulled in the rocking chair. It was nothing less than a little taste of heaven for Abdus. At this moment, he felt complete. He had Abeedah and now Drona. His empty world was soon filled with two epitome souls. It was enough for his immortal life. It was just the first day of rest of their lives.

With little Drona, Abdus and Abeedah had to bid farewell to their sleep, at least most of the times. Sometimes Drona wrestled at night with the dark, and sometimes the daylight tried to comfort him. He was trying to cope up with the new insights of life. Meanwhile, Abdus had started feeling contented with his sleepless nights. During these hours, he decided to make Drona sleep and comfort himself with thoughts and memories of the past.

Time. What is this strange thing called Time? Is there any way to crack its code? Humans have found a way to travel through Earth's orbit, a way to breathe under the water, to fly in the air and to escape the burn from fire, all have been discovered. Only time never revealed her mystery. It has the power to watch and listen to everything. It is our secret keeper until the time it wants to. We people assume that time is always in our hands, but the real fact is that time always have us at its fingertip, just like karma. Time and karma are like sisters. We all are their puppet. Since the biblical times, people have been afraid of Gods and goddesses. It is because of the fear of their wrath, people worship them and try to impress them hoping to get their blessings.

But in actual, all our prayers and worship should be of karma and time. People should be afraid of it because they are extremely powerful. Even Gods and Goddesses have to surrender their power in front of them. They always work together, and the world has to end their knees in front of them. They ensure adequate balance in the environment and the only unbiased law of nature.

Chapter eighteen

Usual life of unusual family

Time has its own way of revealing what really matters to us. What stands on our side is to decide how to appreciate it. Abdus and Abeedah were having every single moment of happiness with their little Drona. It is the truth that the bad times make our life heavier. It refuses to leave us and instead it creates a black universe around us. When it comes to good times, it flies with a blink of eyes.

Little Drona was growing fast. He had eyes of his mother and strength of his father. He had the spirit of his mother and lividness of his father. A few years back, he was just crawling. A few years later, he started taking his first step holding Abdus's finger. Abeedah could remember vividly, the day when she held her arms to him and he held her back.

Drona started to march towards her just like flower blooms after winter. He lifted up his little feet and laughed holding it up in the air. He had a terrific smile which was enough to charm anyone. He then placed his feet hard on the ground with the intention of shaking it. He took three tiny steps and then fell. Having a warrior's blood flowing inside him, he stood up again and took furthermore step. Soon he grabbed his mother's leg to stand a little longer.

"In the upcoming days, you will be walking alone, bravely. You will be wandering on several paths but always remember that I'll always be there to save you from the fall," she said and hugged him tightly. Abdus, keeping all his power and immortality aside, was living a life of a soft-hearted father.

Drona was a night owl which worried his parents, but slowly and steadily they got used to his habits.

Abdus and Abeedah kept turns to watch over him the whole knight. Without disturbing his co-curricular works, they checked on his by peeking from the door. But Drona had strong senses like his father; he always knew when they came to check on him but always presented to be induced in his work. He spent his nights covered under the blanket, reading the comics of his favorite superhero under the subtle light of his toy torch or playing with the little white mouse, he named 'Tutu.'

Other times they found him sitting near the window staring at the city light and stars, repeating the things he learned at school to Tutu.

He only had four to five hours of sleep daily because of which his vision started fading soon, and at a very tender age, he had to take the help of spectacles to see things clearly. As the power of his spectacle increased his creative instinct increased too. He was not like normal child who was surrounded by their little friends at school. He barely made any friends at school. The only name they heard from his mouth was Subodh, who was his bench mate. By the age of five, his room was filled with many crafted toys and walls were covered with modern arts which were beyond anyone's understanding.

While walking towards the school hallway, Abdus and Abeedah saw some colorful paintings on the wall. Food spilled, noodles stuck and even names engraved here and there below four feet. A classmate of Drona was running in the hallway. Abeedah stopped him and asked "Subodh stop! Stop! Where is Drona?"

"Aunty, he is in the common hall," he replied and ran towards the main gate.

They crossed two to three classrooms where few seniors were standing tall and proud with a sense of confidence and experience. On their way to the common hall, she saw some empty classes one of which had a board at the top of it written as 'V- A.'

"This is Drona's classroom," she said and stepped inside the door.

The classroom had a glimpse of childishness. Lunchbox was thrown here and there. The blackboard was full of names and unrecognizable images. Even those wooden benches were not spared from the fine arts of the students. Abeedah started walking from the first bench towards the last seat but stopped beside one and asked Abdus to look at a small corner of the table. It was written Drona and Tia inside a crooked heart-shaped structure. Abeedah giggled and said, "Your son has already found a daughter-in-law for us."

"At least he didn't have to wait 5000 years!" Abdus and chuckled at her.

They entered the common hall. It was all crowded. There he was, sitting with his quiz mates on the stage. Drona was a handsome young child with curly black hair and chubby cheeks. He was wearing his navy blue and white school uniform. His forehead was covered with curly black hair and eyes with his nerdy spectacles. But his chubby cheeks and pretty pink lips where enough to make him look cute. He was looking no less than some prince! He was not fat but was a foodie like his father. They were late for his quiz competition; they managed to enter the hall by the time when the winner was supposed to be announced.

"The first prize goes to the greenhouse! I would like to call upon the team member, Drona, and Kevin." His principal announced.

Everyone applauded for them. Across the crowd, Drona spotted his parents, and in excitement, he waved at them.

"Sometimes when I see Drona, he reminds me of Manik. He was like a son to me." Abeedah sensed Abdus was missing Manik through his eyes. After all these years they still haven't been able to find Manik. As if he had vanished from the face of earth completely. Rajat was devastatd but had been using all his money and resources to find him.

"Where ever he is, he is fine." Abeedah placed her hand on his shoulder and tried to comfort him.

I t was a typical Tuesday morning for an unusual family. Abeedah and Abdus were getting ready for the day. She was trying to wake up little Drona for the school. Drona loved sleeping. He loved it more than food because falling asleep was the hardest thing for him. He used to have an over imagination, and that was a reality in his dreams. He believed in everything, and after living an unbelievable life, his parents never asked him to separate his imagination from reality. Most of the times it was funny, but there were times when his over imagination used to annoy people around him.

"Wake up Drona," she said patting his head.

 She opened the curtains of his room letting the sunlight in to bless his son with its warmth. Soon the light extended itself to the blanket. Drona covered his face to avoid the sun.

"Wake up otherwise you will be late for the school"

Reluctantly, he uncovered his face from the blanket. He blinked and had his first sight of the day. He dragged his feet off the bed and rubbed his eyes. Stretched his arms above his head and yawned, "Good morning mummy."

"Good morning Drona. C'mon fast. Get ready." she started arranging his toys scattered in the room.

"First you force me to sleep and then again force me to wake up, it's confusing what to do?" Drona said innocently.

Abeedah chuckled at his innocent words and said, "If you won't wake up then who will eat the breakfast and who will go to school?" She said and went to the kitchen.

While they all sat for the breakfast, Abdus said, "I have some good news to share today."

Abeedah and Drona raised their eyebrow together as a reflex to it.

"Today it's been three years since we started Drona Archery Academy and I am thinking of expending it. I have already found a partner!"

"Who?" Abeedah asked in excitement.

"Mr. Rajat, Manik's father. He also wants to sponsor a scholarship in Manik's name."

"That's great!"

Drona looked at them and asked curiously, "Who is Manik, papa?"

"Manik was your father's first and favorite student," she replied on behalf of Abdus.

"Was? Is he dead?" Drona asked innocently.

Abeedah deliberately changed the topic. "Eat fast. Your father is getting late for his work" she said childishly and left for the hospital by kissing both of them goodbye.

Seasons are never constant. They come and go just like some tourists visiting a place for the time being. It carries the fragrance of the past and promises for the future, but Abdus had lost the count of seasons he had lived. Travelling around the world, learning different languages and culture kept him busy all those years. Whenever he left any place, he knew that he would never see those people again. Winter is the only season which always made him feel alive. Icy air was forcing its way into the lungs and turning the breath colder. Winter acts as a sensation of pinching someone to wake him up from his daydream. When the chill touches his body, his teeth clatter.

This time, he feels happy to believe that although he is immortal, one day his body will decay and would diminish in the soil. Although Mumbai's winter had its own charms, he had loved winter with snow.

Abdus left Drona at his school gate and watched him getting inside. He was watching him when he saw him talking to an old man halfway. They seemed to look familiar and comfortable with each other. Since that old man was inside the school, Abdus assumed that him to be a staff. The old man was telling Drona about something he did wrong, and he wasn't supposed to do. After what happened to their first child, he and Abeedah were overprotective for Drona.

At the same time, Abdus found it absurd because he was just a nine-year-old kid and kids need their freedom as much as they need protection. Abdus looked at his watch and realized that he was getting late. He took the first gear and pushed the accelerator of his car.

He had purchased an empty gym hall which he had turned into a giant hall for archery. Though it was not lavish, but its four walls and a roof had all kinds of necessity. The student count was growing every month. It was amazing to see the response to this traditional art which was nine thousand years old.

Abdus liked one peculiar thing about human psychology. People are swift in their endeavors to accomplish incredible discoveries, but at the same time, they still are holding on their roots. He leaned towards the door and watched his students practicing, carrying their bows and targeting the red circle. He stepped into the hall and said, "Today we will learn another ancient archery technique that is speed shooting by using double arrows."

"Grab two arrows at once, nock and shoot one while holding the other in the same hand. Then quickly nock and shoot the second one," he explained by demonstrating the technique. He took two wooden coasters from his table and threw it in the air and shot two arrows towards it consequently. Within a difference of less than a second, both the wooden pieces got stuck to the front wall with separate arrow piercing it from the center.

"Hello Abdus" he heard a friendly voice from behind. He turned back and saw Rajat.

"Keep practicing." He said to his students, Passing the bow to one of his students, he welcomed Rajat, "Rajat! It's good to see you here."

"I was just passing by and thought of delivering some good news," he said.

"Sure…" he pulled a chair for him.

"Well, I won't be sitting. I had a conversation with the owner of the store next to the Academy, and he is not ready to sell it but we can at least place an offer. It will be perfect for the expansion. Also, I don't think he would quote much higher as the store is closed for years and by his voice, he sounds very old."

"Okay, let's meet him. The sooner it is settled, faster we can start working on it," he said delightedly.

They got into Rajat's car and headed towards Chembur.

Chapter ninteen

Friend or foe?

After searching the store owner's address for around thirty minutes, they found a bungalow with a name board, Ujjawal Rawat. It was a lavish bungalow with a swimming pool and a garden. The bonsai trees lined the perfect lawn in their wooden boxes. The grass has been mowed so short that the ground was easily visible.

"Okay, I didn't see this coming," said Rajat skeptically raising his eyebrows.

It was large, indeed, almost a dauntingly bungalow. The paintwork on the trim was in white. The windows weren't large enough but indeed a fashionable one. The floors were polished in concrete, and the furniture was tasteful, high-end designed. Many decorative items were antique. It was a glorious mix of cultures and fashion through the ages. An old lady invited them in and asked them to be seated

"Mr. Ujjawal Rawat?" Rajat asked.

"He is taking some rest. This is about?" the lady asked gently.

"Ma'am we are here to discuss your Kurla west store..." Rajat said humbly.

"Please wait," she said and went inside to inform his husband.

After five minutes, she returned and said: "We are not willing to sell our store."

"But it is closed for a decade, I guess! We are making a reasonable offer for it," said Abdus.

"Sorry, I can't help—"

"Wait!" They heard a quaking voice back from the room. Oddly, a Chinese old man in a wheelchair came out of the room. He had fossilized hair, sullen eyes, and parched skin.

"I am Ujjawal Rawat," he said with a blunt look.

"Hello sir, I was saying—" Abdus started making his point when he was interrupted.

"I know you. Your voice... it's too familiar. But how is this possible you haven't aged a single day?" Mr. Rawat said with a curious surprise on his face.

"I don't think so, Mr. Rawat. I am meeting you for the first time" Abdus said while hiding his nervousness.

"Yes, probably I am paranoid. At this age, I tend to forget everything. Sometimes I even forget that I have a wife. I might have mistaken you for someone else who is probably dead." He said with a sudden change in expression.

"You have a lovely house here." Rajat complimented.

"Everything I have is because of that person only," he said with gratitude in his voice.

"I am guessing there is an interesting story here," Rajat said to extend the communication and to build a trust.

"Yes, indeed. We lived in a small town called Xining in China near Huangshui River. I remember vividly. It was 22nd May 1927. Me, my mother and my father, we woke up in the morning and got busy with our usual work when I heard some metal bucket rattles like a freight train just passed. Immediately, everything around started falling, cracks appeared on the ground beneath. Fear and panic followed the ground shook up as if the entire place will fall apart from its usual place.

The cracks, with a speed of a lightening, reached to the nearest building and its bricks started falling upon the people. I saw many people dying right in front of my eyes. My father ran toward us when out of the blue the whole building fell over him. I saw him turning into the pile of crushed bone and muscle in front of my eyes. But I guess it was not our time yet, out of the dirt fog, a large man came to our rescue. He saved me and my mother's life and took us to a safe place. He has injured himself, covered in blood, but he protected us with all his power.

I don't know who he was. Maybe it was my over imagination being a child, but he was not an ordinary human. He had enormous power. At a point, I believe I saw him lifting a heavy broken wall which was about to crush many people. We lost everything in that disastrous earthquake. That generous man took out a ring from his middle finger and placed it in my hand. It was so big that I couldn't cover it in my fist. He asked my mother to use it and start a new life.

That earthquake lasted for less than a minute, but it took thousands of life. Only handful of us managed to survive. For a while, we lived in Nepal and then we found our refuge here. I kept that ring in my pocket for the whole time, and it was a large golden ring! We never knew that its worth was in millions.

At that time, India was under the rule of Britishers. Under the brutal behavior and proud nature, they also had an excellent sense of valuable things. For some reason they called it some Ring of Gyges and offered us gold coins and lands in exchange. My mother married an Indian man. She changed my name, and since then this place is our home. It's been so long that I barely recall my original name, but I can never forget his voice. "

"Such a fascinating story Mr. Rawat" Rajat was impressed. Abdus was still hiding his nervousness behind his poker face.

"Indeed it is. When I heard your voice and saw you, I thought….But how is it possible? You look even younger than him… Anyways, why are you here?" he stared at Abdus.

"I own an archery academy, and we want to expand it. We wanted to make an offer to you for your store." Abdus explained politely.

"Oh! Take it," he said bluntly.

Rajat and Abdus looked were quite surprised at his reply. They were confused and looked at each other.

"I don't want anything in exchange. Just take it. I mean, I am over a century old neither do I have an heir to take care of it. The store place stands useless for me. Eventually, I am going to donate everything as I feel that my death is not so far..." he said in a casual tone unaware of his wife giving him a cold look.

"That is very generous of you Mr. Rawat." Rajat lifted his hand to shake on the deal but Mr. Rawat was too old and weak even to raise the grip on his own. Rajat apologies and they left after drinking their last sip of coffee.

Abdus reached home with a smile on his face and. Today, he was nostalgic. He saw Abeedah and Drona sitting on the couch; she was helping little Drona with his homework. Abdus walked up to them and sat on the empty sit of the sofa, Drona jumped in the excitement of seeing his father. Abeedah made him some coffee and sat again with Drona. She asked Abdus about his day which was always answered in either 'Fine' for the normal day and 'Good' for better days. He always spared the details for the bedtime whenever he had anything exciting to share. Abeedah then informed, "Drona's teacher wrote a note in his school diary. It says that our son is brilliant and they want him to participate in Math Olympiad where he will be representing his school."

Abdus felt proud, and congratulated Drona by showing him his favorite chocolate. He ran toward Abdus and sat on his lap, which was a sign that he really had a good day.

"My little genius!" Abdus hugged him tightly and went to keep the coffee mug in the kitchen when he saw a coffee stain on the slab. He took a piece of cloth and started cleaning it while Abeedah was talking to Drona.

"What about Subodh, is he also participating?" Abeedah asked.

"No, he is stupid and fools. He never completes his homework. We are not friends anymore!" Drona replied cruelly.

"Why are you saying that? Friends are friends, no matter how they are!"

"No mom. Friendship can never survive between a poor and a rich man, between a man of letters and an uneducated mind, between a brave and a coward."

Abdus, who was listening to their argument, left that piece of cloth on the slab, walked back to the drawing room and asked suspiciously, "Those are some heavy words, little man…who taught you that?"

"We have a new librarian teacher at the school, Acharya sir. He teaches me many good things. He is quite old, but he is my friend." Drona smiled gleamingly.

Abdus assumed that he might be the same person with whom Drona was talking to this morning. "Indeed he is teaching you excellent stuff, but you are taking it in a wrong way, son. Roads are made for you to move forward but choosing the wrong path or right will always be your decision. You should never underestimate anyone neither you should consider yourself superior. The moment when a person considers himself superior from others, at that moment, he is a fool," he said wisely.

Drona realized his mistake and apologies for the behavior. For him, his father was the role model of his life.

Few days later while he was at the academy teaching another ancient technique, when one of his students informed him that his phone was ringing continuously.

"Hello… Am I talking to Mr. Abdus?" a female voice said over Abdus's phone.

"Yes, it's me. May I know with whom I am speaking to?"

"This is Mrs. Chandrika Rawat. My husband had asked me to call you. He wants to sign the store papers today itself."

"Okay. Sure, ma'am. I will be there for a couple of hours. How is Mr. Rawat?"

"He is not well. See you then!" she hung up the phone.

Abdus reached their house by 2 PM. There was a pin drop silence in the house. He looked here and there and then he called for Mrs. Rawat. She came out of her room with a doctor. She looked worried, and the doctor looked severe. She saw Abdus and asked him to settle down while she drops off the doctor to the gate.

She came back after few minutes and asked Abdus to follow her. She took him to Mr. Rawat's room where he was lying partially dead. His face was pale just like his soul was ready to leave his body slowly and steadily. Mr. Rawat, through his actions, indicated his wife to leave the room.

Then he pointed his fingers towards a drawer and asked Abdus to take out the papers as he had not much time left in this world. Abdus took out the documents and handed it to him with a shiny silver pen. Mr. Rawat was quite eager to sign the papers as he knew beforehand his time of death. After signing the documents, Abdus took the pen from his hand and placed it on the blanket. He adjusted his pillow to make it more comfortable for him.

Mr. Rawat waved his finger to call him closer and started murmuring something which was barely audible. Abdus moved his ears closer to his mouth to hear what he wanted to say and then in his last dying breath he said, "I know that was you. Thank you." he closed his eyes. The ECG machine, which was attached to his body, displayed a flat line. His soul had finally left his body.

Abdus felt a strange form of sadness for Mr. Rawat. He was the first person in all his years that he got to see twice. He no longer had a warrior's heart which was not bothered by the loss of life. For him, death was never a casualty. By now, he had understood the essence of a human life. It is to serve the humanity, being compassionate and to always help others.

It was past 12 AM. Abdus came home with grief in his heart. He took off his jacket from his tired shoulders. Slowly, he took off his shoes which was squeezing his feet more than any other day. He hung his blazer on a hanger and went towards the kitchen to find something to drink. He took a pint of beer and sat on the couch, trying to let go of his exhaustion. He felt something beneath his seat and found some paper crafts lying which got flattened due to his weight. One by one, he took it out and started restructuring it to the previous state.

Gradually, he was getting high and murmured to himself. "It's true that when a man walks a mile on a hot summer day that too on a dusty Indian road, then only he will understand the reason behind the invention of beer." He took his first sip from the green bottle and could sense the path he was going down. While he was restructuring the craft, he saw something was written on it.

Curiously, he unfolded the paper and got stunned. "He is coming for your son!" This was written on the paper, but the fact which shocked him was that it was written in Ravyank language. It was a secret encryption language developed by his uncle Kripacharya during the war of Kurukshetra to exchange the encrypted strategic notes amongst the Kauravas. The writing was tough to decipher, and the pan was to transmit the message without getting noticed by the enemy.

It was next to impossible to crack the code because each code had different key to crack it and couldn't be done without the knowledge of the receiver's name. Other than High rankers of the Kauravas, nobody was aware of this language.

Goosebumps bloomed on his arms. He unfolded all the craft, and there was this same message written over and over. His bottle of beer fell from on the floor. Pin drop silence was replaced by the echo of a glass clinking on the tiles which shattered on the floor. He ran upstairs into Drona's room. Abeedah got up with the noise and saw him running towards Drona's room. She ran behind him.

He shook Drona hard enough to get his answers, "Who gave you this?" he showed that craft paper.

Abeedah got scared with his behavior. "What are you doing? Stop it!" and grabbed his hand. She read the goose bumps on his skin like an old blind man read Braille and asked him to calm down. She had an intuition that something was wrong.

"Who gave you this?" He shouted again.

"Acharya sir…" Drona got scared by seeing his father in such a furious state.

"What happened? Will you please tell me?" shouted Abeedah.

In agitation, he came back to his room and threw all the crafts on the ground. Abeedah and Drona had no idea of what had just happened.

He couldn't sleep that night. Staring at the slow circulating fan with an unstable heartbeat, he passed his night somehow squeezing himself on the couch. He never wanted to put Abeedah and Drona in any danger.

By morning, he was eager enough to meet this teacher. It was 5:15 AM. He left his home in a rush without informing anybody. Abeedah woke up at the creaking sound of the door.

He sat on the wooden bench outside the school. Eyes stuck on the gate; he frequently watched his wristwatch to check the time. After three hours, the school gate opened and he rushed into the principal's office.

"Hello Ma'am, I am Drona's father, Abdus."

"Yes Mr. Abdus, you have a brilliant son!"

"Ma'am, I want to know about Mr. Acharya."

"Who?"

"Mr. Acharya, the librarian."

"Oh yes! He is a wise man and indeed an intelligent one. He had recently joined our school as a temporary replacement for Mrs.Sangeeta. Unfortunately, he resigned yesterday." she informed courteously.

"Can I see his picture or get his address?"

"Well, we do maintain records of every teacher. I can help you with. Is this for Drona? They seem very close to each other" she asked.

"Yes. Drona wants to meet him…" he replied in a stammering voice.

She searched for Mr. Acharya's record thoroughly but couldn't find it.

"I am sorry, but it seems like his record file is missing." She searched the whole cabinet and didn't find his records.

Abdus's suspicion grew stronger on this man. He turned towards the door and started walking, after taking four to five steps, he stopped and asked the principal "What happened to Mrs.Sangeeta?"

"Unfortunately, while going home from the school, she was hit by a car and hurt her leg. Not much injured but she is suggested for a couple of month bed rest to remove her plaster. The very next day Mr. Acharya came to us looking for a job."

Immediately Abdus understood that it was all a setup. He came home, and he knew that only through Drona he could contact him. One thing he wasn't sure about was, who was he? A friend or a foe?

Chapter Twenty

Humanity has found its station

Mumbai. People call it the city of dreams, they also say this city never sleeps but it doesn't scream either. There was something about this city which couldn't be ignored, and it is defiantly a place where dream does come true. People know how to live and find peace in the choking humidity, rushing paths and where traffic in the streets is chaotic. It was amazing to see how humanity has found its station.

The city is a Zion for many people, a land surrounded by seas where millions live in harmony. Where rich people spend their evening in five-star hotels, others find their ideal seating on the seas shore. Rollers of gem-blue dashed the sand beneath the tuft clouds of the wizard- white drifted past in the sky like a curtain of silk with their loved ones in Marin drive instead of shedding blood for what they lack. Beyond the horizon, the sun illuminated the shimmering haze of pollution.

In the far distance, the silhouette of the skyline pierced through the warm glow like a jagged mountain ridge. Millions of lights caused the dense mass of skyscrapers glitter. People are needle points, and cars are blood cells flowing through the veins of the city. Despite the time, the hustle and bustle never came to a halt.

After traveling half of the world, Abdus also found his Arcady here. Walking on an esplanade and feeling the cool breeze was something that keeps his lividness behind the wall. He walked for hours and hours on the boulevard passing by some palm trees. He bought a newspaper from a small boy, and Mumbai's famous cutting chai and sat on the two steps concrete stairs watching the tetrapod dissipate the force of waves and Started reading the front page news.

Gang attack in British libraries

"A new gang is channeling their terror by attacking the libraries in the United Kingdom. On Tuesday night they trespassed the British Library and the Bodleian Library. The authority has confirmed that nothing but two manuscripts of 'The Book of Soyga,' also known as Aldaraian was stolen.

The book of soya is 16th- century Latin treatise on magic and more, which was known to have been in possessed by the Elizabethan scholar John Dee. After Dee's Death, the book was thought to be lost until 1994. It is one of the oldest books of humankind. It is said to have been presented to Adam himself by the angels of God in the Garden of Eden. It is noted that the 197 pages of the book consist of everything from spells rituals and information on other magical demonology and astrology.

It is also said that the book contains the secrets of the underworld. But the language is still undefined. The CCTV footage confirms that the robbery was done precisely at the same time in both the Library. Is it for money or some satanic worship? Police are still lacking any hard clue on the robbers."

England, United Kingdom

A lavish hall surrounded by the circular wall. With numerous paintings on the wall from archangel Micheal holding his sword to Lord Ram holding his bow, from the Greek god of war Ares to furious Hindu God Shiva, from Aphrodite the goddess of fertility, love and beauty to the destroyer of evil forces goddess Kali, one of the foremost goddesses of Norse Frigg to the flamboyant God of light Apollo. Amongst all these, there stood a statue in white with no face engrave. The whole room was describing the power and belief of the high power man with the beard standing near the window watch outside the window in a grey suit. The aura of the place was pleasant.

Three handsome men Jilus and Abigor, clean-shaven, suited up and Rick with stubble beard wearing a pink shirt and trouser entered the room in style. They were Cambions possessing a human body. They were offspring of a Demon father and human mother, a supernatural creature filled with all sorts of powerful black magic.

"Brother Chrone we brought you a gift," Jilus said placing both the manuscript of Aldaraian on the circular table in from of him.

"What about Roanoke Codex," Chrone asked.

Jilus, Abigor, and Rick looked at each as they had nothing to display that could please their adamant brother.

An advent entered the room with codex in her hand. She was Vila named Malia. Vila is the Slavic versions of nymphs, who have power over wind, which they delight in causing storms of high winds, she is an Omni lingual maiden who bear no specific face or body of her own. She is just the reflexion of desires of the person looking at her because her primary motive is to seduce. Her voice was as beautiful as the rest of her, and could form large gusts of winds that can lift houses into the air. Despite their feminine charms, however, she was a fierce warriors. Chrone possesses a piece of her skin, due to which her loyalty lye to him.

"Here it is," she said keeping it with other two books on the table.

"I knew I could count on you Malia" Chrone praised Malia.

"How did you get it?" Julus asked curiously.

"It was available on Amazon," said Malia which made Rick laugh.

Chrone touched the codex with a smile on his face and said "Ved Vyas is the only person who can read the book of Sogya. He wrote this codex which is the only key to read the spells written in Aldaraian." holding one of the books in his hand walked towards the statue "Father you don't have to wait long to walk on the earth. I have watched you burning every year. But this won't happen any anymore. I am your failsafe." said looking at the statue.

"Don't you think this dress is little seducing" Rick whispered in his Scottish accent to Malia, teasing her.

"It's not the dress; it's my body, which is seductive. If you are feeling jealous, then you should have possessed a woman's body. Not this junky" she viciously replied back.

"How are we going to do this?" Malia asked Chrone.

"Where is the boy?" he asked Abigor.

"He is in India, but it will not be easy to get him. He is under the protection of Ashwatthama" he replied.

"Don't forget I am failsafe," he said with wide eyes.

"But why this boy?" Malia asked again.

"Because he is the only one born out of two curses. He is our last hope" said Abigor.

The meeting was dismissed. Abigor, Rick, and Malia stepped outside the room leaving Julus and Chrone in the room. Abigor being the smartest one engaged himself in cracking the code while Rick trailed Malia to her car, whom he was attracted to. Malia besides throwing him shades and bickering, she also enjoyed his company.

"Chrone's obsession will kill us one day" he sat in her car's passenger seat, intending to start a conversation with her.

"Then why are you helping him?" Malia asked while starting the car.

"Because we are family. A family is who you survive with when you want to survive even if you don't like them. That's what family does. Though I have never seen him, I want my father as much as he does. Mother, told us he was a wise man and a great king."

"A demon is a demon," she said taunting him.

"In a way it's true but being a demon does mean they are intended to do wrong." He replied thoughtfully.

"We!" she corrected him.

"What?"

"'We' not 'They' aren't you one of them?" she taunted again.

"No. I am not a demon I am Cambian. I just have the supernatural power of a demon because of my father but also have my mother's soft tender heart, of course with wings. You know little perk of being a child of cross breed." He flirted.

She rolled her eyes and pushed the accelerator of her car.

Meanwhile, Julus stated his concern about Malia to Chrone, "I don't trust her brother, and I would suggest you should not trust her either."

Chrone chucked and said, "I don't trust anyone but my brothers. I know her. She is loyal to me till I have her skin. We have a deal. She will help us in bringing back our father, and I will return the favor by reuniting her with her family. Let bygones be bygones; we need her now. On the plus side, she is a good pawn."

He looked at Jilus who was still not convinced and continued by placing a hand on his shoulder, "If it feels like she is double-crossing us. We can always burn that skin, and she will not be the problem anymore."

"And what about Rick, he seems distracted. I don't think he is onboard with our plan" Julus said again.

"Rick has a young heart. He the youngest and we must protect him. He sees the world differently. He still has so many things to learn. Don't worry about him." Chrone replied, getting back to work on to find out ways to bring his father back.

Chapter twenty-one

Can't help falling in love with you....

Lying on the bed, head partially resting on the pillow, her long hair scattered all over the bed. Holding bun stick in her right hand, she stretched her head twice with it and then placing it in between her canine teeth. Abeedah wrote Stuffed Pomfret fry on her dairy. She was deciding the menu for the evening party. Today was their 15th wedding anniversary. Her cell phone beeped, she received a text message from Abdus.

"Get ready; I will pick you and Drona at sharp 7 PM."

As promised Abdus called Abeedah to come down at sharp 7 PM. Abeedah was wearing the red satin gown, his first gift to her and Drona looked like a little corporate man in his suit and spectacles. The moment he saw Abeedah in the dress, it was like watching at her for the first time. Drona was walking with her holding her hand towards him; there was completeness inside Abdus.

The celebration was a riot of color, everyone a little more hyped up than they should be. A smile painted on their faces and a glass of wine in hand. On the request of Abeedah Dj played the song "Elvis Presley's - Can't help falling in love" and asked him for a dance. It was the same song which was playing on the television the day they expressed their love to each other, she wanted to recreate those particular moments all over again. Abdus was not a dancer but everything about the flowing silks made him dance, his feet moved with grace and heart beating with joy. Their bodies moved together as they celebrated, rhythmically breaking into shapes and colors that tickled their nerves.

Everyone present at the gathering was enjoying it in their own way. Some sat on the bar, amused by liquor, debated on various universal topics, while others were enjoying their time out of work. For ladies, every party is a gossip gathering with expensive jewelry and designer dresses. Only children knew the actual meaning of a party, and they were experiencing unrestrained joy in their play station. They created a space which was feathers and sparkles, smiles and laughter.

Abdus looked around and saw the real meaning of the celebration. Shad's parents, Rajat, Mrs. Harshwardhan and little Ryan who was not so little anymore, and their little made up family of friends and colleagues they made up in the years. He recalled the day when he felt the same happiness, the day when he was crowned as the king of Northern Panchal. He remembered how much he wanted to celebrate his joy with his father and mother both on his side, but bound by the society and tradition which did not allow women of the noble family to join such celebration which involved wine and dance. Parties and celebrations were only for men and forbidden or considered taboo for women. It was fun, but it was far from happiness. Today, he saw man and woman equally standing and celebrating together. He thought to himself, "The time has changed, and so does the mindset of people."

In the middle of music, debates, gossips, and laughter, Abdus clicked his glass, twice.

"Excuse me! Excuse me!" he said clearing his throat.

"Thank you every for coming to this party. I want to thank my wife Abeedah for creating this evening wonderful."

He took a deep breath, softly chuckled and said, "'My wife' whenever I say this two words together, I feel to be the most powerful person in the world. These two words together remind me that I am not alone. You cannot make every single day a happy day but one single happy day is worth waiting. You cannot laugh the whole day, but the only smile makes the entire day worth suffering. You are that smile for me. You have given me the happiness, which I don't think I deserve and with Drona, it feels like a dream from which I don't want to wake up, no matter if I die in sleep. I never thought I would see this day. Abeedah, I cannot promise you that we'll take our last breath together, but I promise you that I will love you till my last breath."

Abeedah stood with tears in her eyes, loving every single word coming from Abdus and blew him a kiss as everybody around them clapped for Abdus's beautiful words for Abeedah.

The party concluded with a perfect family picture of Abdus, Abeedah and little Drona, which they hung on the front wall of the drawing room beside Abdus's record collection. A family of three with delusional past and prodigious future, living in the perfect present.

This family of three had many things to worry about, but they wake up and indulged themselves to work, with hugs and kiss their day starts. One beautiful day, Drona being as stubborn he is, using his over imagination, created a treasure map and started collecting the little hints and clues that he designed himself. Unaware of the fact that he was getting late for the school, he kept himself busy in solving mysteries. Half shirt unbuttoned, messy curly hair like tangled noodles, ran with a sock in one leg and other barefoot. Unaware of the consequences he broke the expensive lamp with his wooden sword, making his tie an eye patch he ran in search of gold.

Irritated with the noise, mother shouted: "Stop it!"

Drona stopped at once.

"Can't you see the clock? You are late for the school." she scolded him.

She brought a comb and pulled him close. Annoyed, she started untangling his hair. At the back of his head, she saw some black spots and his veins turning dark near the area. Worried, she observed him carefully but couldn't find anything suspicious. The mother's heart got concerned but she assumed it some kind of flue. With troubled mind, she left for the hospital. She found it hard to concentrate on her patients the whole day. At evening, on her way back home, she brought a couple of test-tubes to collect Drona's blood samples for some tests.

Drona was preparing hard for the Olympiad. Although he was one of the smartest kids in school, he was naive too. His dedication was creating chills for his parents. Slowly his hard work was showing on his face. Under his eyes started circling by darkness. The power spectacles were increasing rapidly like mercury. Worried sick about his heath they asked him to withdraw from the competition but Drona was adamant. His health was not getting better, even a slight bit. Abeedah was not able to figure out the reason behind his uncertain degrading health. Also, his blood samples needed a week for the result.

The day of the Olympiad exam arrived. Drona was all ready with his sharpen pencils and a pen.

Seven hours later, Abeedah came out of a surgery and switched on her cell phone, immediately, she received a call from his school, his principal informed her that his son has collapsed during the assembly and they have admitted him to the city hospital. She sat down on her seat.

The evening was chilly, but her blood was icy, and her muscles turned tense. She rushed towards the door faster than the rain touches the ground and hopped on the first cab she found on the road. On the way, she tried to call Abdus, but her shivering hand always pressed one-one instead of one which was his speed dial number. After the fourth attempt, she heard it ringing.

After hearing the news, Abdus reach the hospital in no time, brown and dull like all the others and saw Abeedah sitting beside Drona. Doctors and nurses surrounded his hospital bed, attaching IV's, heart monitors and oxygen tanks to him. The bed was set low, and Drona was laying on it, unconscious, his eyes sunken and his skin pale like the blood is being soaked from his veins. His ear was continually dropping blood turning the white pillow red. His veins near the near the neck and wrist was turning black. The doctors didn't know what was happening to him, but as procedure, they had a list of tests done on him.

Abdus was pleased to see the silver hair on the doctor from a distance. When he turned, he saw her sage face and bipolar glasses. She was the same doctor who delivered Drona. The moment she arrived into the sheep white room, he gained a slight faith that his son was in right hand. But the doctor was also not much of help. Unaware of the sickness the only thing they did was injecting him with various drugs.

They couldn't do anything else but wait.

The wait turned to days, and Abdus's lividness was crossing the wall. He was amazed to see himself holding up his anger so well. He would have spilled blood by now, if such thing happened back in his day. It was becoming harder and harder for them to see their only son lying on the bed for this long. Whenever he rests his eyes sitting at the corner of the room in a brown hard leathered couch, he imagined Drona playing with his little wooden sword and poking him to listen to his unrealistic alien stories.

Abeedah on the other hand, had faith in her karma. After what she experiences with his first child, she firmly believed that her karma couldn't pay off this way. She thought that this was just a temporary suffering and soon his beloved son will wake up and say, "Mummy where are my glasses?"

Abdus made that brown couch his temporary home. His eyes rested briefly on Drona. Tired enough he stretched his legs and rested his head on the arm of the sofa, looked out the window. It's been more than a week he hasn't seen the sun. It was almost sunset. The yellow ball of fire changed to hues of orange, and then almost tangerine. It was merging with the sky, like rum dissolving in a glass of water. Silhouettes of birds flew home across a sky.

Abdus looked at Drona's face with affection and love and then turned towards the setting sun. Then he prayed. He prayed to one of gods he knew, who never abandoned this earth and turned his back on it. He closed his eyes drowning himself to calmness, releasing his veins from all the stress and prayed for his son. It is indeed said that love can melt a rock.

Under the blanket of stillness, he closed his eyes resting his faith on time. He felt the presence of someone in the room and opened his eyes. He saw Abeedah standing near Drona touching hand gently.

"Abeedah!" he said.

She looked at Abdus with a terrified look.

"Don't be afraid, he will be fine?" he said to comfort her.

"You have been here all day long. Go outside take fresh air" she said calmly.

"Yes, you are probably right," he said and stood up.

"You stay with him. I am going for some coffee." He said and started walking toward the door. Halfway he stopped and came near Abeedah kissed his forehead and said "I will be back soon." and left.

He stepped outside the hospital, looked left and right and then took a deep breath stretching his arms and walked towards a nearby café then decided to get latte with extra sugar for take away.

"Good evening sir! How may I help you?" one of the waiters in green apron asked with a gentle smile.

"Just a latte for takeout with extra sugar please," he replied.

The waiter nodded and started pouring coffee into the disposal cup. Abdus took the first sip of the coffee and felt the energy reaching his numb limbs through the warmth of the fluid flowing through his throat; he looked outside the glass door of the cafe. A beautiful black Ferrari was standing outside the hospital.

It's not every day, you see Ferrari on the road," The waiter said.

"Yeah, right. Lucky man, he must be" Abdus said wearisome and handed him hundred rupees note.

"No sir, she was a woman. In fact the most incredible and beautiful woman I have ever seen" he said.

Then he saw Abeedah coming out of the hospital, wearing a tight black dress which was weird for him as Abeedah mostly wore jeans and casual tops. She was holding Drona in her arms. He felt cranky seeing her like that, and when he saw her getting into the Ferrari, he was surreal and left the cafe in a rush, his coffee left on the counter.

He shouted "Abeedah, wait!" repeatedly.

Ignoring his calls, she left in the car with Drona inside. Divested, he ran behind the car, but with a blink of an eye, the car speeded and disappeared quickly. All freaked out; he called Abeedah's cell phone, which he wasn't expecting that she would pick up the call but with the second ring she answered.

"What are you doing? Where are you taking Drona?" he said breathing heavily.

"What? What are you saying? I am at home cooking dinner." she said.

"What?" He was aberrant.

"What happened to Drona?" she asked worried.

He was too shocked to reply or inform anything to Abeedah. He lost his guts and was unable to deliver her the news that his beloved son has been kidnapped. He was sick to his stomach and didn't know what to do next. He looked left and right, took a cab and reached the nearest police station.

"I want to file a report, my son is kidnapped," he said to one of the incharge seating on the front desk, sipping tea from the cup. The policeman instantly placed the cup on the table and asked him to calm down and describe the whole situation.

Abdus, himself was confused about what he saw, was in a dilemma to narrate the story. It was incomprehensible to him too.

"A lady kidnapped my son, from the hospital. In front of my eyes." he hassled.

"Can you give us the description of the lady?"

Abdus saw his wife Abeedah, but he was confident she wasn't the one. Hence he was sure that she was something or somebody else. So he lied.

"No sir, it was dark so I couldn't get a glimpse of her face, but she was driving Ferrari, a black one."

"Sir, we cannot file any official complain now, but I will personally send my men to look for your son" he informed.

"But he is in the coma."

"Sorry sir, we cannot do much as of now."

Abdus couldn't accept such casual response for his son. He lost his anger and hit the policeman hard enough which made him hear the sound of bells in his head. With the second hit, the policeman fell on the floor hitting his head badly. Everyone at the station ran towards him, stopping him with all their power from every side possible. Abdus realized he had made the stupidest mistake at this crucial time when every minute counts.

They threw him behind bars. After begging for couple of hours the lady constable understood his situation and allowed him to make one phone call. At that instance, he knew he has to do everything on its own now without losing much time.

A friend in need is a friend indeed they say. He called Rajat and asked for his help. Rajat in a heartbeat agreed and reached the police station as fast as he could. Rajat being a businessman had contacted with high ranked officers in the city. He made couple of calls and within an hour arranged Abdus's bail.

Chapter twenty-two

Calling the demon

Abdus told him the whole story, skipping the part where he saw Abeedah taking away Drona.

Rajat said, "The only way we can find your son is through technology." He said it like some low profile detective.

He took him to a hacker named Aditya. He lived in a crappy place surrounded by fish market. He could smell the stink of fish half a kilometer before they reached his house. The street was so narrow for the car to get in. So, they parked it on the main road and marched all the way to his small, messy, stinky flat. He lived in the third floor, to which stairs were the only rout. Rajat being thin passed by easy but it created trouble to Abdus to pass by with such giant physic. He brought his shoulders closed enough pass through it and reached to the third floor. The floor had only two doors, and it was easy to guess for his.

Abdus had spent a century of his life in a dark pit but that pit was even better than this place, he thought to himself. Rajat introduced him to Aditya. A shaggy guy, hair all messed up, wearing a round neck t-shirt with un-patterned design, jeans all torn up. He young and would probably be in high school. One could assume that he takes bath once in a week. Abdus could smell the marijuana in his house, and his eyes looked dizzy and tired. He was high. He whispered in Rajat's ear "I think we are in wrong place. He doesn't look like the guy we are looking for."

"Don't get to the conclusion easily; he is the guy we are looking for. Although never judge the gift by its wrapper" he patted Abdus.

They asked him to track down the black Ferrari using the surveillance cameras. He wrote something gibberish on his laptop, and they saw the video of the moment where Abeedah was taking Drona.

"WHAT!" Rajat reacted strangely.

"What happened?" Abdus asked curiously.

"I know her."

"Yeah, she is….." Abdus said.

"She is Shivangi, my assistant. But why would she kidnap Drona? I mean she is a nice girl."

Abdus chuckled at Rajat, and now he understood the whole mystery. He knew she was neither Abeedah nor his assistant Shivangi. She was Vila. After two hours of nonstop programming and following the car, camera by camera, Aditya tracked down the black Ferrari.

"Man, I found it." He shouted with excitement.

Rajat and Abdus, who were trying other sources to find out, ran towards Aditya.

"Where it went," Abdus asked.

"From the hospital, it directly went to Taj hotel, and it is still parked there."

They thanked Aditya by paying him whatever money they had in his pockets.

"Can I ask you one thing?" Rajat asked.

"Yeah sure anything man."

"You can make the easiest money I have ever seen. Then why are living in such a crazy place."

"Yeah of course I can. But last time I hacked the police records to clean up the record of my past crimes, and I was caught. Since then I am on their radar. The owner of this flat doesn't want any ID proof or any contract. He is just concerned with his rent. If anytime thing goes south, I can just pack up and run, with no traces of mine left behind. This is the perfect hideaway for me." he explained and turned his executive chair towards his laptop.

"Please, close the door on your way out," he said and again started typing something gibberish.

They saw the black Ferrari parked on the loft. The hotel was lavish in fact the most lavish hotel in Mumbai, which had a certain protocol for their guests. As Abdus was not in proper dress code. He waited near the loft and Rajat went inside to inquire.

"Excuse me! Can you please tell me the owner of the black Ferrari?" He asked the receptionist at the front desk.

"Sir those are our taxi cars, provided to our A-listed customer." She replied.

"Can you tell me the name of the last person who took the car?"

"Sorry sir but we cannot disclose our official data to anyone."

"No! No! It's not like that. The lady who was in the car, her bag was exchange with mine. I just wanted to return it back."

"Oh! In that case, last it was rented by Mohini Sharma. But she checked out a few hours ago." she replied.

"You mean like the actress?" he raised his eyebrow.

"Yes!"

"Are you sure? Do you have any ID or something?"

"No Sir, unfortunately, she wasn't carrying her ID, but she was with a man. I can give you his name."

She checked her computer and wrote a name on a piece of paper and passed the paper to him, which he slid into his pocket.

Rajat came out of the lobby and showed the piece of paper to Abdus. It was written

'Chrone Millar. Contact number- +91 80********'

Abdus all confused and sad crushed the paper and took out his phone from his pocket. 36 missed calls and 44 messages, All from Abeedah. He opened the last text message and read.

"She found out about Drona" he informed Rajat. And disappointed in himself, he sat by the side of the road.

"Don't worry we will find your son. I won't let the same thing that happened to me, happen to you. We have enough proof to start our search. I will call the commissioner." Rajat consoled Abdus.

A beedah was continually trying to contact Abdus, tears shredding continuously, she was pissed and confused. Finally, she decided to take things in her own hands. Scared inside, she took her car keys and left a final voice mail to her husband,

"This is your wife again. I know you are worried too, but this is not the time to sit and grieve. I want my son back. I am going to police station to file a missing report. I hope you meet me——"

In the middle of her voice mail, she heard the doorbell ringing. She assumed it would be Sumeet, her colleague, whom she called to accompany her to the police station.

She opened the door and saw a man standing.

"Who are you? How may I help you?" She asked

"Oh dear, I am your well-wisher." He replied.

"Sorry, I think you are at wrong address?"

"Oh no Abeedah, I never make any mistake," he said and touched Abeedah's side temple with his two fingers and she collapses.

Abdus returned home to check on Abeedah. He stepped each stair, terrified, searching answers for Abeedah's question in his mind. Also trying to find a valid reason for Drona's kidnapping. He put the key at the door lock, but the door was open. He entered and switched on the light of the drawing room. Then he saw her cell phone tossed on the floor.

The site panicked Abdus. He knew Abeedah is a strong but fear just need a crack to find its grip in some one's heart. He searched the whole flat, but there was no sign of her. anywhere. Immediately, he called Sumeet. He knew Sumeet is her confidant and oldest colleague she trusts. But when he confirmed that he was supposed to meet her, but he was stuck in traffic for three hours. He felt devastated more than anger. He went on the road and asked every person walking by about Abeedah, showing her picture, but had no luck. He felt that this was a way of punishing him for expecting a real life after being cursed for eternity. He couldn't think straight.

It was a complicated mystery that needed to be solved. Pull out the crushed piece of paper from his pocket and saw the name again. He went to Aditya but this time alone. He placed the piece of paper with force on his desk beside the laptop and asked him to provide every single detail; he can fetch about this guy.

"Man, tracking a car is one thing, tracking a person is whole another. It will cost you more," he said casually.

Abdus's eyes turned red, which was a sign of his anger and he pulled him up in the air with his collar and threatened him "More than your life?"

"Ok ok man put me down. I will do as you say." He was scared to death with his extreme power.

He landed on the floor and started writing something gibberish again and after half an hour. He said "I couldn't get much information, but this is how he looks. But if we are lucky and the GPS on his phone is on we can get his exact location."

"Please do it fast," Abdus said.

He types few codes and smiled, "Yes, we are lucky, his GPS is on, and right now he is in a restaurant called Little Italy."

"I will pay you well. Just keep me updated about his location" he said and left in a rush.

On the way, while he was driving really fast, he received a call from Aditya.

"Yes, what is it?" he asked.

"He is on the move; he is going towards Colaba market."

He took a turn and sped up his car and reached Colaba in no time. Parked his car near the ATM and started looking for Chrone and he found him near the antique clock store glazing at a vintage pocket watch. He ran towards him and like some angry bear, jumped over him, punching with his giant fist on his face, again and again.

"Where is my son and my wife," he asked curiously.

"Your son," he said sarcastically and laughed "You will never find him, Ashwatthama."

He froze on hearing his name from Chrone, "Who are you?" was the first question that arrived in his mind.

"You cannot hurt me; you are just hurting this vessel," he said and laughed again.

His anger turned to rage, and he gave him fist after fist. Abdus was uncontrollable. A police patrol car came on the spot and tried to stop him. But he was not an ordinary man who could be arrested easily. It took four policemen to calm him down, by the time he regained his senses back, Chrone was gone.

For the crime he committed, the police turned him in, again. He spent the whole night at the jail. One way or other this night of Abdus was meant to be in jail. He realized this is not Panchal, he was neither Aswatthama nor the crowned king. He was a family man now living a normal human life. Here he cannot let his anger go out of control. He has to tolerate things because his actions will bring unwanted consequences. He passed the night cursing and blaming himself for what happened to Drona and Abeedah. He knew, everything was happening because of who he is.

Chapter Twenty-three

Apollo is watching you

Next day Rajat came to the police station and paid for his bail, again. He was the only person he could count on under these circumstances. More than forty-eight hours passed and he hasn't had any clue about Abeedah or Drona. There was a feeling of failure, and powerlessness that was growing inside of him, every minute passing by.

On the roadside, he saw a bar and went inside because at this time alcohol was the only faithful companion which could provide him comfort and calmness. He sat on the bar counter, where the bartender was serving the order with his impressive art of juggling. He sat quietly and ordered neat bourbon.

While Abdus was sipping his whiskey watching the news telecast, the music started with a hymn. On the small stage, six feet tall man was sitting on a stool in front of mike with a guitar. He was freakishly handsome with drop-dead Greek-Indian striking looks. His hazel green eyes, a stubble beard, and golden-brown curly hair attracted every single person sitting on the bar. He had a body of a supermodel. Graphite slacks showcasing his powerful thighs. His white shirt was halfway buttoned revealing his clean brown chest with black blazer complimented the fedora on his head. A man too perfect to be a human, started singing "Cliff Richard's - Dady's home." It was like a siren's enchanting music to every ear it reached.

The singer finished his song and crowd giving him a roaring applaud. He walked towards the bar counter in a lazy swagger and sat beside Abdus who was drowning in his sorrow.

Thinking about the tragedy of his life the news on the small television hanging near the bar counter caught his attention as hi sipped his whiskey.

The news anchor was saying, "Today on his speech at white house, The President of America said, "We will not let the refugees and outsiders rule our country, it belongs to the Americans. We will not let them nest over it."

Abdus after hearing the news chuckled sardonically, said to himself out loud, "Yeah, as they took it back from the Indians."

The handsome singer sitting beside him heard his words and asked in confusion,"Indians?"

"I mean native Americans. Usually, they are called Indians." Abdus explained.

"Like one of those animated character Pocahontas, right?" He asked.

"Yeah, but she is not just an animated character. She was a real woman."

"Oh, I remember her, beautiful Matoka. Not just outside but beautiful inside too. Poor girl suffered a lot. It was her mother who was Pocahontas, who was also really beautiful. His father used to call her Pocahontas after her mother." The stranger said with a faraway look on his face.

"How do you know about this?" Abdus asked incredulously.

"Son, I know I look so youthful and dashing, but I'm older than you."

"Older than me, Yaah, right. Who are you? God!"

The stranger shook his head and did not reply, a secretive smile on his face. Abdus knew that he was not going to get a reply from him. Being someone who has avoided conversations his own life, Abdus understood when he wasn't going to get answers, and kept staring at him.

"Is something wrong?" the singer asked, looking back at Abdus, smiling.

He shook his head, smiled dull, and raised his glass "By the way, Great performance."

"Yes, I know it was," he said self-proclaiming himself.

"Every lady in the bar is drooling over you, and every man wants to be you."

"Well it's not easy to get this look, I have to burn myself for this," he said sarcastically.

Abdus completed his drink, paid and got up from his seat. The man grabbed his hand and persuaded him to seat a little longer. Abdus irritated with his action said, "Look. I am not in a mood to have little chat."

"Then let me accompany you with your loneliness. I have a long experience in that area."

"You expertise in loneliness? Yeah, right! Buddy, just leave me alone." he said sullenly.

"Okay, it's your call. Unless you want to know about your wife and your son" He removed his hand and said.

"What? How do you know about that?" he asked suspiciously.

"I know everything that happens in my watch." He answered skeptically. "Let's just walk out. The music is too loud here."

He threw money on the table, Abdus followed him out. They stood on the street sideways.

"I know where is your son and the motive behind his abduction," he said.

While they were talking a man was walking down the sideways but being blocked by two men he shouted at them "Move aside."

"Are you talking to me?" the singer asked with his nose on air.

"Yes, both of you. MOVE"

The singer touched his shoulder pushing him to walk ahead and said "My apologies" after walking few steps his shoulder started burning which within few second reached his limbs and he fell. It took ten steps for him to turn from a walking and breathing body to a burned up corpse.

Abdus saw this happening in front of his eyes.

"Did you do that?" he was stunned.

"When a fly buzz too much, he has to be gone," he replied casually.

"But humans are not flies."

"Yes, my apology. Comparing humans to a fly was an insult to the flies. You little human have ruined everything, including me. God created you last of all because he needed something to protect and nourish his beautiful creation like a gardener. But instead, they started destroying everything for their greed and comfort. I can finish them off in a blink of eyes but what I did? I just watched this happening. Why? Because I am an obedient son of my father. I perform my duty turning my eye blind. There will come a day when I won't tolerate this anymore. Humans are the best example of artificial intelligence, which went wrong. God should have never given them such power."

"Who are you?" He asked adamantly.

"People call me with many names Malakbel, Tenerife, Meri and many more. In Indian, I am known as Surya Dev, but I prefer to be called Apollo. You know it sounds strong, powerful, masculine, and more substantial, it suits my personality. Surya dev is like people didn't have much time to find me a name. You know how it feels? It feels like I am not important to them. No extra effort. It makes me sad." he said.

Abdus just stood there staring at this person who was complaining about how humans worshipped him. He recovered, focusing over the information about his son.

"Where is he?" he pleaded.

Rather than telling him about Drona, he said, "Ahh! The love of a family is one of the life's greatest blessings bonded by the most powerful fluid in the world, blood. You know why blood is red? Because red color represents power. I'm in love with red. I think it's such a passionate color."

Ashwatthama unaware of the sense behind his words asked again, "Please, will you tell me about my son."

Apollo, "Have patience and listen to me and one more thing I don't like to be interrupted."

After creating a dramatic environment, he continued, "The most harmful and foolish kind of prejudice is prejudice against yourself. A blood relation is the most durable and everlasting connections. The person you are genetically connected with, you will always be connected no matter how far or close you are. You are not a normal person Ashwatthama. Your blood has immense power. Concentrate on the power that follows in your blood. It will defiantly take you to your son."

"And where is Abeedah?" He asked.

"Oh don't worry about her. She is safe with me. It's time she needs a little awakening."

"You have her? What awakening? Where is she?"

"Do you think you are the only special person with a fascinating story?"

"I asked you where is she? Take me to her."

"She is safe and you will meet her, but it's your son who is in danger and needs you. Now close your eyes and look for your blood."

Abdus closed his eyes and concentrated on Drona and let himself dragged to his subconscious state. His body was still standing with Apollo but his subconscious mind travelled, he opened his eyes and saw himself sitting in a restaurant where he saw a gleam of blurred images, and then he closed his eyes again. Then he saw himself standing in the middle of the road still everything was blurred, he closed his eyes for the third time and when he opened, he saw himself standing at the doorstep of an old house outside Mumbai. This time the vision was clear; he read the address on the wall which says Mr. and Mrs. Lokhande, Villa#5, Hill View Street, Lavasa.

His subconscious mind could pass through the door with opening it. His presence was like a ghost, to which no one could see. He stepped inside and saw two men sitting in the drawing hall playing chess, and the drawing room was surrounded by four bedrooms and a open kitchen. He moved forward and saw Vila wearing Abeedah's face making sandwiches, which she kept on a bone china plate and walked towards the first room, Abdus followed her. There he saw Rick who was unknown to him; Vila and Rick looked cozy, he left them in their mood and when to the second bedroom, where he saw Chrone sitting on the study table and marking something on an ancient book. Abdus got so angry looking at him as if he would rip him apart, but he couldn't even touch him as he was in his subconscious state. Then called Drona's name twice to remind himself his primary aim and his surname calmed him down. After which he moved to the third room and saw Drona lying on a bed, alone unconscious. His heartbeat quickened and he opened his eyes.

"I saw Drona. I know where he is." he said.

"I told you." Apollo smiled.

"But why have they abducted Drona? What is their problem with me? I don't even know them."

"They are not taking any revenge. They are resurrecting their father's soul in your son's body." he said.

"What! But why my son?"

"You know a curse is more powerful than a boon. His body is a very powerful vessel for a powerful soul. Only his body is strong enough to hold such power in it."

"Whose soul are you talking about, here? Who was their father?"

"The soul of my dear friend Ravana."

"Ravana!" he felt sick on his guts, it was too much to process for him, "but Drona is just a boy."

"No, he is not just a boy. He is the culmination of two curses." Apollo explained patiently.

"Two? You are mistaken here. I am the only cursed parent of Drona."

"No, Ashwatthama you are not the only cursed soul in his life," Apollo said skeptically.

"Oh so you know now" They heard a voice from their back. They turned and saw Mrityu.

"What are you doing here? Don't you have some duty to perform?" Apollo taunted Mrityu.

"Well, I saw you canoodling with Ashwatthama here. So, I thought it might be a public holiday." Mrityu replied sarcastically.

"You two carry on with your insults. I have a son to find, but Abeedah?" Abdus looked at Apollo.

"You don't worry about her. She is safe with me." Apollo said looking at Mrityu. "I promise I will return her safe after I am done with her. Go save your son."

Abdus waved his hand in the air, calling for a cab when he heard.

"Wait!" Apollo said, "I want to give you something."

"What?" Abdus asked.

Apollo held both his hand from the wrist tightly, and a yellow, red incandescent light flew through his veins and reached his palm, burning his skin. When the burning glow went dull, he saw a bow drawn on his left palm and a shield on other.

"What is this?" he asked.

"Karna was my favorite son. He always made me proud as a father. I know you didn't like him much but then also, you saved his life on the battlefield. As a token of gratitude, I am blessing you with this magnificent powerful Pinaka Bow which I reconstructed with my divine power after Rama broke it, to fight your foe and Medusa Shield to protect your family. I know you will need this in future because there is a greater war coming, bigger than Mahabharata, where I hope you will follow the path of Dharma.”

“War?” Abdus choked.

“You can't expect rainbow without little rain” Apollo replied.

Abdus thanked him and went to the nearest car that was parked, broke the lock and drove away, towards Lavasa.

“That was a touching moment” Mrityu was witnessing the whole conversation standing by their side said sarcastically. “Now tell me what else did you tell him?”

“Oh, you mean how brutally you murdered his unborn child or about your plan of killing Drona?” Apollo eyebrows rose in taunting manner.

“You know this is in everybody's best interest.” Mrityu replied miffed.

“Every ones? Or yours? I see you are afraid. You are afraid that Ravana will join the army. That's why you don't want him to walk on earth again. Isn't it? ” Apollo teased him.

“Are you mad? Yes, I killed Ashwatthama's unborn child but Drona. It wasn't me. I think you need to cool down a bit; you are too hot on your head.” Mrityu said furiously in denial.

“I see everything. I saw you putting that poison on Drona's lunch. It was a deadly viper's poison, it could have killed a normal human within a zap of fingers, but Drona has a strong body and adamant soul. It is taking time to spread.” Apollo said.

“Okay fine. Yes, I did this, and yes I am afraid of thinking the unthinkable. Even if Ashwatthama finds him, he will die. His soul will not hold him long. There is no escape.” Mrityu said.

Apollo grabbed a lady's attention walking by looked into her eyes, like he was hypnotizing her with his dreamy eyes, “You know what the beauty of the future is? The beauty of the future is that it is unknown, even to me. I see everything, even beyond the parallel universe but I am still not sure about it because it keeps on changing every instance. It changes with every actions and decision, one make. One can predict it or call it faith, but no one is sure about it.”

“Will you go on a date with me?” he asked the mesmerize lady.

“Yes,” she said and blushed.

“Mexican or Italian?”

“Italian.”

“Ahh! Le Pain Quotidien, my favorite. Let's go” he said seductively.

Mrityu rolled his eyes at Apollo.

“You know where to find me. But don't bother, I insist” Apollo said to Mrityu sarcastically and waved him bye.

“Arrogant” Mrityu murmured and walked in the opposite direction.

Chapter Twenty-four

Chants are power

Abdus fed the address on the GPS and started driving towards Lavasa at the speed of 130 Km/hr. He had to reach to Drona as soon as possible. It was night and road was pitch black with no street light, and he could just see the path few hundred meters ahead, till the car's headlight allowed him to. On the way, he crossed his path with five other vehicles, only. He stopped at the lamppost near the old house. A security guard was standing at the door to block the outsiders who tried to prevent Abdus as well from entering the premises. He put his hand hard to Abdus's chest, threatening him not to enter the house.

But Abdus was not a normal outsider. He punched him so hard that he crashed the door and was thrown inside breaking it into two pieces. His white shirt turned red; his skin was torn from many places in his body making the ribs visible, his should dislocate. But the guard was also a hard man to put down. He pulled his strength to perform his duty and crawled towards Abdus. Abdus bend in his one knee and with his rock-solid fist smashed his skull.

Abigor came out upon hearing the commotion and saw the smashed head of the guard, which looked like smashed red velvet cake with an eye floating on it. Abigor was a high maintenance man with dignity on his shoulder. He gave Abdus a real fight, and a warrior who was shield by a father's heart found a window.

When Abigor was losing his strong fight and strength, he pulled up his supernatural power. He flipped his shoulder, and a pair of golden wings grew on his back with tips burning on fire. His eyes turned yellow, and his skull was partially visible from his skin, which was his real face, a face of cambion filled with black magical powers. He struck Abdus like a storm during thunderbolts, one after the other. Abdus wears an immortal body, the flashes hardly scratched him but slowed him down pretty good.

He prayed for the Medusa shield to appear for his protection, but he wasn't aware of the way or chant to enable it. He now knew he had to put an equal fight which is more than some fist punch. He closed his eyes and let all the six senses in his body while Abigor continued hitting him with all he got, and Pinaka bow with a glow appeared in his right hand, it was an unbelievably enormous bow with tightened by hundreds of thread strangled. He closed his eyes again this time to pray Lord Indra and chanted for his powerful Aindra Astra.

As he completed his chanting a divine arrow appears, nocked on the bow. He honored it with his gratitude and empowered it by pouring his strength. He took his aim towards Abigor and released the string. First, his wings started burning which reached his spinal chords burning him inside out as he screamed, leaving a pile of black ash behind on the ground.

While, Abigor went outside the room to fight Abdus leaving Malia, Jilus, Rick, and Chrone behind with Drona, Chrone was holding the book of Soyga and Jilus was holding the codex. Every great spell needs blood, needs sacrifices and this spell needed one too. Jilus who had an unshakeable trust in his brother Chrone voluntarily offered himself for the sacrifice.

Rick felt devastated inside and out, seeing his brother sacrificing himself for a father they didn't even know. Chrone, on the other hand, was thinking south. He had big plans after the resurrection; he didn't bother how many lives he had to sacrifices pursue his strategy. More than his father, he wanted his power, he wanted his terror to raise a world, where they don't have to hide behind a vulnerable human body, a world where they don't have to hide their precious power, but people bowing down to them.

"Brother I don't think this is a good idea. What is the meaning of calling a father we haven't seen by sacrificing our brother who walked with us shoulder to shoulder all these centuries?" Rick pleaded Chrone.

"You are just getting cold feet, brother. Don't worry about me. I feel privileged, sacrificing myself for the one who brought us into this world." Jilus replied on behalf of Chrone.

hrone patted Jilus on his should and said: "Our father will be very proud of you."

Rick felt disgusted with their behavior. Flipped his shoulders to get his wings and flew away towards the dark and dense forest through the large window in the room.

Chrone ordered Malia "Go get him; he has the piece of gem."

She jumped out of the window like a ninja and followed Rick to the forest.

"Abigor won't be able to hold Ashwatthama for long; we have to start the ritual now," Chrone said.

They heard the scream of Abigor, and both rushed to the drawing room and saw their brother turned to ashes. They flipped their shoulders and transformed to their true forms. Chrone was powerful among them all. They both attacked Abdus with their black magic; they attacked him with their magically spelled bullets, each bullet was carvel with spell and symbols. As they stroke Abdus's body it started numbing that body part.

Abdus's body began losing its strength which let the bow off its power, and it started vanishing from the tip and emerged into his palm but Ashwatthama still had enough strength to tangle Jilus with his arms. He wrapped his arms around his neck pulled him on the floor and started chocking his throat. Then Chrone pulled a pendant off his neck, it was not a regular pendant, magical pendent CIRCA and throw towards Abdus which sticks to his chest, which starts sucking all the power and strength in his body making him weaker and weaker. He falls on the ground and his vision begin blurring. Suddenly somebody throws the gas bomb inside the room, which makes Chrone and Jilus unable to see anything.

An old man enters the room and pluck the circa from his chest and throw it toward Jilus. The circa starts sucking power and strength off Jilus. He helps Ashwatthama to stand on his own feet, but Ashwatthama unable to see the face of the old man, heard a voice "Stand son, your son needs you."

Abdus again chants for the bow, this time he prayed the Nagas, the presiding deity of Naga Astra and shoot Chrone. The arrow took the shape of a snake and wrapped around Chrone which blocks his wings to supply power to Chrone. The snake then bites Chrone with its venom. Abdus ran towards Drona but before he could save him. Bitten Chrone crawled into the room and said: "If my father cannot arise, I will not let your son live too."

He chants a powerful spell making a fireball in his hand and threw it on Drona. Abdus in a rush didn't know what to do. He put his arms around Drona and Medusa shield appears on his wrist for his protection. Medusa's eyes turn Chrone into stone. Amazed at the power of Medusa shield, Abdus looked up and thanked Apollo for blessing him with the guard and protecting his beloved son.

He grabbed Drona and brought him out of the house. He looked for the man who saved him, but nobody was there just Jilus lying aching with pain on the floor. He heads out and see Malia and Rick standing in front of him.

"Stop else I will kill you both," Abdus shouted.

Rick pulled back Malia and said "Take him, we will not stop you. We never wanted to hurt your son. I am apologizing on behalf of my brothers."

Abdus kept Drona on the car and drove towards home. Drona's veins almost turned black. His dying skin made his father's heart ache in pain. He continued blaming himself for everything that was happening to him and Abeedah. He was convinced that he wasn't supposed to be happy, wasn't supposed to have a family, he wasn't supposed to get peace. He dreamed of all those things and thought he could leave a normal life like another human being in a normal world. On the way to home, he imagined all sorts of alternative life that Abeedah could have lived if she had never met him. Drona would have never been born. That would have been the best thing because being never born is better than going through the pain of death.

CHAPTER Twenty-five

Abeedah's awakening

Apollo saying

Every life is beautiful and vital. Some are born to serve their duty, some to finish the unfinished business, some are born because they are blessed, and some are born because of their curse. Abdus is not the only cursed soul in this story. Everything happens for a reason; even a simple mosquito bite can change some part of one's life, it rains because of a cause and these reasons brought us here. Everything around us is butterfly effect. Though it's a theory for humans but from where I see, it is a fact. But until the truth is revealed, the reason is unknown. Also, showing the truth before its time is useless.

Truth has magnificent power, a power that can take everything from you and skill that can make you something. So we must make it feel special. The truth I am talking about is the truth of Abeedah, of her existence, of her being attracted to a person whom she was once terrified to look at. Why after suffering for 5000 years, all of a sudden his wounds mended. How Ashwatthama got his redemption after her touch. All questions will be answered with this one truth. Her story takes us not so far for me but seventh Century B.C. Roam.

Abeedah wakes up in a beautiful garden. There was a gate of rough wood was as big as a cow and ivy cascaded over the fence, growing tendrils in every direction. The stone path was evenly punctuated with weeds after every stone like some decorative items. The disheveled, un-manicured lawn was more moss than grass and was overshadowed by substantial weeping willow flowing down onto the moist and squishy ground. Clusters of defiant daffodils reared their golden heads amidst the gloom, and there were matters of fuchsia alongside the scarlet and saffron-hued primroses. There was a circular lawn with a path around it.

There was a central bed of shrubs. Outside of the lawn area were four rose bush beds to fill up the square space. Tangled thickets of thorn, flower beds, disheveled lawns, tangled hawthorn, summer greenness, knotted boughs, branches drooped dankly. The one side boundary walls was partially visible due to the series of apple trees in front of it, bend down due to the weight of the fruit. Abeedah looked around hesitant. The grass beneath her hands felt soft as velvet. The smell was refreshing. It was a soothing site for her eyes. She was confused; she wasn't sure that she was in Mumbai anymore.

Then she saw Apollo sitting on the park bench. "Ahh! Finally, you are awake?" he said. He walked up to her and offered his hand.

She stood up on her feet, brushing off the leaves tangled in her hair, looked around and asked "Who are you? Where am I?"

"I told you, I am your well wisher. You are in my secret heaven. Whenever I get tired or sad, I sit here, watch these beautiful flowers blossoming. "

Suddenly she recalled the abduction of Drone and recalled the last thing she was doing; she was going out to file a complaint.

"Why did you bring me here? I have to go. Drona —,"

"Don't worry about him, he is with Ashwatthama."

"How do you know his real name? Who are you?" Shocked Abeedah asked Apollo.

"Oh me?" he sighed and continued with swagger, "I know everything. I am sick of giving my introduction again and again. I am Sun God; you can call me Apollo."

"Is this some joke. Am I supposed to laugh here? If this is a prank, I don't care if he is immortal, I will kill him."

Annoyed Apollo said, "People this day are so reluctant to everything that they won't believe even when a God himself stands in front of them. They complain again and again that Gods have turned their back towards them. It's like asking for the miracle without even believing in the existence of magic."

Abeedah still couldn't make herself believe in his words because she had an image of Gods, which was like serious, using balanced words, all dressed up as mythological characters showed in movies. But Apollo was nowhere near that image. Though he did have looks of Greek God with his dirty blond hair and beautiful face, she was having a hard time believing that he is an actual God with the way he was speaking casually like a bored college student. He is looked more like an actor with would play a God.

"You are no God. You don't look like a God."

"This is my mortal vessel. Humans cannot bear to see my original form." He replied.

Apollo plucked a rose from his garden and with a touch of his finger, burning it to dust. "Now you believe?" He asked.

"My apologies. I didn't mean to disrespect you." She pleaded, "How is my son, Lord. I want to see him."

"He is with your husband but also few steps away from Death. He has been poisoned," he replied.

"Please save him, I beg you."

"It is not in my hand Abeedah, but it is in yours."

Abeedah looked clueless and asked "How?"

"Abeedah I want to tell you a story you will find your answers in this story, will you visualize it for me." He said this like he was some director of a movie, making a frame with his hands.

She nodded and listened to him carefully.

"Far in the city called Urbs Sacra that means —"

"The Sacred City" Abeedah translated.

"Exactly, six girls between the ages of 6 to 10 were chosen by the Chief Priest, all representing the daughters of the royal house. They were chosen to become the priestess, who tended the state cult of Vesta, the goddess of the hearth. They pledge to serve the goddess for 30 years, during which time they had to remain virgins.

Afterward, they could marry, but only a few did. They were called the Vestal Virgins. They lived in the House of Vestal virgins on the Roman Forum near the temple of Vesta. Their duties included tending the perpetual fire in the Temple, keeping their vow of chastity, fetching water from a sacred spring, preparing ritual food, caring for objects in the temple's inner sanctuary, and officiating at the Vestalia, the period of public worship of Vesta. Failure to attend to their duties was punished by a beating; violation of the vow of chastity, by burial alive because the Romans considered them of such high regards that they believed the blood of Vestal Virgin could not be spilled.

Apart from all the rules and duties, they had many honors and privileges too. They even had the power to free condemned prisoners and slaves. A condemned man on his way to his execution only had to catch a glimpse of a Vestal to be freed. "

Abeedah interrupted, "Is this a story or giving me a history lesson?"

"Oh! This is just the background now shush." Apollo said.

He took out a thick, wide book from the small pocket in his blazer and continued, "There was one special girl, Aurelia Romilia. Young Aurelia was just eight years old when she first wore a white infula, a white wooden suffibulum, and a palla. She was Vesta's favorite."

Abeedah interrupted again, "Are you reading this story from the book? Because your eyes and yours words are not coordinating with each other."

Apollo raised an eyebrow and asked, "What?"

"I mean you are barely looking at the book."

"No, I am not narrating the story from the book."

"Then why are you holding it?"

"It just seems more compelling with a book in hand." With an annoyed look, he closed the book hard enough to make it slamming shut and said, "Now don't interrupt." He took a deep breath and continued.

"She cooked delicious food delicious ritual food and served his duty which her hearth, no matter what. She daily brought a rose for the goddess Vesta and placed her on the floor near the fire, and when she comes back with the ritual food, the rose was never there. She worshiped Vesta with all her heart.

When she turned 12, she received a letter from her father that her mother was no more and he was getting married again to a woman from Venice. Whose father was the pearl merchant? He wanted her blessing for the marriage. Aurelia's heart broke, but she provided blessings to her father for their marriage and continued her duties and worship. Cecilia, Aurelia's stepmother, had two younger brothers, Augustus and Pietro who lived in Rome with her. Augustus was immature, arrogant, condensed man. Drunk with the power of money and Pietro was following his brother's path.

Once, Augustus fell in love with one of the maids in the castle. He considered love as possession. He followed her all around the castle. Without wasting much time, he proposed her to be his wife. The maid was aware of the furious and arrogant nature and refused him, stating the difference in their class as an excuse. Augustus's male ego was hurt, and he couldn't take the refusal from a low-class maid, as he was high born.

He chopped off her hands and then her neck, brutally.

As a result, the king sentenced him to execution. The money he was so proud of, didn't play many roles in the judgment. Cecilia loved her brothers as her own children. She couldn't let such death to Augustus. After thinking a lot, she wrote a letter to her step-daughter, the vessel virgin Aurelia, pleading her to pay a visit to Augustus during his time of execution. Her glimpse could save his life. She confronted her that his brother was naive and he committed a crime under the influence of love. Aurelia was a righteous woman, and she never would side with any crime or lie. She refused her request, and Augustus was executed in public.

This action of Aurelia made her so mad. That couldn't see it right through. She blamed Aurelia for his brother's death. She ordered her youngest brother Pietro to rape Aurelia because losing her virginity would lead her to her death. She wanted death for death.

Pietro followed grieving for his brother, found his sister's decision justified and followed her order. He abducted Aurelia while she was plucking the rose for Goddess Vesta and raped her brutally and the fire went out, which was a terrible omen because the fire not only represented the men of Rome but Rome itself.

Romans believed that flames of the fire kept Rome safe and protected.

Indented people of Rome, accused her of breaking her vow of chastity. They buried her within the inner city walls. The Romans used tricky language to make it seem the Virgin Aurelia was not buried because she was not dead when she entered her tomb. The girl entered her small tomb which contained a few provisions, and she was left "not to die." She was assumed to break her vow of chastity, was cursed by Goddess of Vesta, that she will not go to Elysium after her soul leaves the body rather she will take birth again and again and live a life filled with pain.

Miserable and down hearted Aurelia prayed the one God, she worshipped after Goddess Vesta, Apollo. Apollo that is me, I knew everything that happened to her. Because nothing escapes from my sight, no matter how thick the walls are. For those who don't know me, I am a righteous person too. I paid a visit to Aurelia in her small tomb. She was petrified not because of the curse but for what she was accused of.

A curse is a solemn utterance intended to invoke a supernatural power, which cannot be undone even by the mighty Gods or Goddess. But I altered it a little bit with my blessing. I blessed her that she will go to the Elysium. When she love someone more than life, that she could sacrifice herself for his life. Her sacrifice will lay down the veil, and she will be released from the curse.

You heard the story. Now close your eyes and visualize and tell me what do you see?"

Abeedah closed her eyes for a brief moment. He saw a blurred reflection of a small girl wondering in a beautiful castle. She saw her mother trading her golden brown hair. Her father tucking her in the circular bed, which was surrounded by blue drapes. Then she saw a young girl wearing a white dress like some saint. The harder she tried more briefly she could see her actions and her surrounding but not her face until she saw the fire of Vesta burning like a graceful woman dancing in the rhythm of the air blowing towards her. She opened her eyes, occupied dilemma, and confusion, she said, "I saw myself. It wasn't my face, but it was me, I know, Aurelia. I am confused."

"Yes. It is your story. You are Aurelia. I mean you are the cursed, reincarnating soul of Aurelia. It was because of your pure soul. That your touch mended Ashwatthama's wounds. Now you know your story. You know what to do." Apollo said and zapped her by touching her head with his two fingers. She found herself sitting on the couch of her house.

Chapter Twenty six

spells and rituals

Abeedah was calm and undoubted. She grabbed her keys and went to the hospital, where Drona was admitted. She entered the room and saw Abdus sitting beside Drona. The moment he saw Abeedah, he ran and hugged her. For a second he was hesitant if she was not Abeedah but Vila. But a human body has more sensitive memory than their brain. Her soft touch felt comfort to him, and he knew she was his Abeedah.

"Where have you been?" Abdus asked.

"I was with —, never mind you won't believe me." She replied.

"Apollo?" He asked.

"How do you know?"

"He is the reason Drona is with us now. It is a long story anyways," he explained.

"That means he was right," Abeedah said to herself.

"What?"

"Nothing," she said and smiled.

Drona's veins were turned black, and he was just hours away from death. Abdus felt helpless to save his son. He felt devastated and failure. On the other hand, Abeedah did not have a single wrinkle on her four head. She looked so calm and composed as if she had a magical spell to cure Drona; in fact she knew one.

Abeedah asked Abdus to look after her son while she went for a walk. Abdus had no idea for Abeedah's bizarre behavior. He though she might be under some trauma which is restricting her to believe the circumstances.

Abeedah removed her sleepers and started walking on the grass. She took her last walk in this world. While walking barefoot, a dried thorn got stuck to her skin, yet she enjoys it because she knew this would the last time, she feels the aching pain, the last time she is feeling the breeze, last time she is watching at the sunlight. The last time she saw The sun rays falling as a blanket of white upon the greenery. In their glow the nascent leaves of spring lie papery and delicate, drinking in the energy the trees crave.

On the ground lies the wetness of a recent rain-shower, soaking into the dark mud. She imagined herself alone until I stop to listen really and look. But today she didn't want to be alone. She tried to take as much as she could from her memory. Only some far away was the ocean, alive with constant motion and millions of sea-dwellers. Beyond this wall of white, I can smell and hear it. The waves are neither the gentle kind that rolls up the beach like an overflowing bath tub nor the crashing kind that turn murky with golden swirling crystals. They move with force but die within a few feet. This last walks in nature, were her treasure because her heart started bleeding as the thought of leaving Abdus and Drona crossed her mind.

He knew the last process of this ritual, but she was not sure about how it would work. Slitting the wrist was the way Drona will get his life back. Thinking of this her heart started beating fast. She touched her heart requesting it beat steadily. Then she looked at the pendent Abdus gave her, saying it had power to resurrect. She was all geared up and with a steady heart and mind went to Drona's room and saw Abdus sobbing over his dying son.

At that moment he recalled his sin of killing Draupadi's sons. He could now feel the pain of a mother, holding her son's dead bodies. It was in that instance he knew the reason behind his curse and his suffering for 5000 years and was convinced that he deserved to suffer, for the sins he committed. For him losing Drona would be more painful than the pain he felt when he lost his beloved father.

Abeedah consoled him wiping his tears, "Everything will be alright, we won't lose our son, I won't let it happen." she asked him to take walk outside, in order to get him away from Drona.

She pulled off the gem from her pendent and placed it in between Drona's chest. Suddenly she heard, "A broken piece won't do you much help." She turned towards the voice and saw Rick standing at the door.

She looked at Rick suspiciously, as he never saw him before and had no idea who he was. "I am Rick, by the way, I am here to help your son." He said while walking into the room.

"How can you help him?" She asked.

He took out the other broken piece of gem from his jacket and kept it near the other piece of jewel on Drona's chest. He placed his palm over the treasure and chanted some spell, which joint them making one complete piece.

"Your son's soul is getting weaker and weaker; the poison has spread all over his body. I can save him, but the spell demands sacrifices," he said. Rick tricked her to bring his father back as he was the only family he could count on.

"I am ready to sacrifices myself for my son's life." She said holding Drona's little hand.

"Okay, then we need to do it now. Drona doesn't have much time in his hand."

Rick kept The Book of Soyga beside Drona.

"Are you sure about it?" he asked Abeedah.

"It is written in Quran, Whoever kills an innocent person…it is as though he has killed all mankind, even if it's your own life." Rick said.

"It is also written - whoever saves a life; it is as though she had saved all mankind." She said looking at Drona with love and compassion.

Rick smiled and opened the book. After turning few pages, he started chanted the spell. Abdus who was standing on the street at the coffee stall felt a weirdness vibe in the air. He looked at the sky and suddenly, the sky was consumed in numerous shades of grey and white and black. It looked like the sun has given up on trying to break through this iron curtain of clouds that it has become content to lounging out behind them.

It was two pages spell with numerous unknown symbols which Jilus and Abigor encrypted using the codex. As Rick completed the spell from the first page, the fragment of in Drona's body starts powering up, and the gem of his chest begins to glow a little. The blackness from his veins began fading away. The spell was working. He looked at Abeedah and singled her apologetically to do what was needed. She touches Drona's four head, pushing back his curly hair from his forehead and with a kiss on it, she said, "I love you so much, baby. Take care of your father and tell him I love him with all my heart." After looking at his son's sweet face for a brief moment, she singled back to Rick that she was ready.

Rick started reading the spell from the second page, Abeedah felt a choking pain on her body, and her soul was being pulled out of her body by the spell. A portal for other side opened, and the vale between both the worlds dropped down for a while. The gem filled with the supernatural power attracted the Ravana's soul towards it. The white beam of light traveled through the portal, which got absorbed by the gem, making it glow like a sun.

Abeedah suffering from immense pain looked at the portal and saw the Reapers for the last time, standing inside it. They joined their sickles together and then she saw her soul leaving the body and going inside the black hole of the sickle with a light speed. Her body fell on the ground, like dead meat. She was dead, eyes fixed and vacant. But her sacrifice worked, there is nothing bigger power than a mother's sacrifice.

The spell and ritual worked performed by Rick worked, Ravana's soul, passing through the veil and was in the gem. Rick held his palm over the gem and pushed the soul to Drona's body using his power. But something unexpected happened. When the portal was getting closed, it opened to its full length for a second causing chaos, heat and disturbance and then closed like instantly.

Abdus while returning to the hospital saw a sharp light in Drona's room. He knew something was wrong. He felt something unthinkable has happened. A flickering doubt already was growing inside his mind, like a mist cloud above the sea, since he saw Abeedah's cold behavior. The coffee paper cup fell off his hand, and he ran towards the room.

Shocked at the view of the room, Abdus stood still at the door, with a throbbing heartbeat, he needed time to process. He felt a stroke inside him when he saw Abeedah lying on the floor breathless. He moved with haste towards her, held her head resting it on his lap and realized that she was gone. He crouched, one hand over his still chest. He picked up her hand, so cold and pale, touching it to his chick, he wanted to feel her touch and closed his eyes for just a moment hoping it to provide the warmth of her compassion, but it was icy cold. He was mute, but the tears were finding its way to touch her lips like the last kiss they never got to have. His mind struggled to stay at that moment. To live every second with her body, convincing himself that the love of his life, has left him.

Rick felt guilt in his heart, taking the love from one's life was the last thing he wanted. This is what he was afraid of all these time, he was an emotional Cambion but also the smart one too. Although he wanted to bring his father back but also had an intension of saving Drona too. Drona was in this condition because of his brothers. He would have failed in his plan if he hadn't tricked Abeedah. He looked at Drona, and his black veins were turning pink, vanishing beneath his skin.

Abdus when saw Rick with the same book he saw in the old house, he busted at him. He held his collar and pulled him hard. Rick thought he was dead today. He needed to persuade him to listen. Otherwise, he was head.

Livid Abdus shouted, "You did this, I am going to tear you apart from limb to limb."

"I didn't do anything, she wanted me to save his son, and this was the only way," he explained.

"You killed her." He touted again.

"No. No I didn't she sacrificed herself. She said this was her faith."

Abdus now understood everything. He realized the reason behind her weird behavior, and he followed why Apollo took her. He fell on the floor on his knees and cried aloud. I was very difficult for him to believe what happened to him. Then he looked at Drona; he looked healthy and sound. He was confused to morn over Abeedah's death or to be happy for getting back Drona's life. He thought he was prepared to feel any pain. But no matter how much you are prepared, losing the person also hit with the same intensity of pain.

The wall clock ticked forwards, he placed her hand on her side and lay with her, feeling her body cold, his tears soaking in her hair. The heaviness was in her limbs as much as her mind. It was more than crying; it was the kids of desolate sobbing that comes from a person drained of all hope. His whole body hung limp like each limb weighed twice as much as it had before and just moving it about was a slow, painful effort. When the words would not come, the tears did. He cried until there was nothing left inside but a raw emptiness that nibbles at his insides like a hungry rat. His irises were threaded scarlet, and his eyeballs hung heavy in their sockets.

Rick kept the gem that belonged to Abdus in his hand and closed the fist. He couldn't watch his pain anymore. He left the room and went down where Maila was waiting for him inside the car.

"I saw the light," she said.

"I don't know if I did the right thing," he said.

Chapter Twenty-seven

Ravana walking earth

Pain says a lot without uttering one word. Everything felt blue and dull without her. She was 6 feet under the ground. But she still held his heart, her memories crushing it inside. He was in pain. How to characterize an unending pain? It's not that difficult. You know you are in endless pain when you wake up one morning and realize that you are dead, buried and forgotten by those who are dear and close to you but alive and kicking to strangers, people who don't give a damn about you.

You know you will forever be in pain when you wake up in the morning, with a jolt, to an emotionless face of someone who tells you nothing but to go out and kill, take another human's life or yours would be taken in more painful ways than you can imagine. You know pain when you go to sleep with it every night, and you see yourself being lowered in your own grave but when you scream to those mourning and burying you your screams are whimpers that no one hears.

Emotional pain leaves invisible scars, yet they can be traced by the most gentle of touch. It isn't felt the way a cut or bruise is. This is far different, and only you can tell it is there. Sometimes the pain is at the back of your mind like a pulse. Occasionally, like a tumor, the "wound" must be opened to be healed; other times a well-meaning person may seek to heal what should be left alone. He tried to reason this unbearable burning but didn't find any. Everything felt so confused, just like a jumbled set of a puzzle. If it can be ignored and a normal happy life resumed, isn't it kinder to have faith in the natural healing process?

Memories were the sole torturer of a man. He couldn't escape them, or hide from them; they are the worst kind of monster. He had experienced pain before, but that was different. This pain felt like somebody was squeezing his heart inside out. At night he could hear her yelling. Voices echoed down the hallway into the bedroom saying "Abdus, I am home." cheerfully, waking him up from his sleep.

Some love stories aren't epic, or doesn't have ever lasting happy endings , or too popular to be given examples for, some a short stories and some are just wrapped inside few lines of poem but it doesn't mean they aren't filled with every inch of deep, consuming love.

He felt so raw today; like there is no skin over his body and the wind makes it bleed. The only thing that is keeping his body alive is his immortality, and the only thing that keeps him breathing is Drona. Who, he wasn't sure, if he was his son anymore. If the little demon remembers any memory that they shared together. If he even remembers the mother who gave her birth, who loved him more than anything till her last breath, the mother who happily sacrificed her life to save his. But Abdus always saw Abeedah's reflection on his face. The same innocence Drona inherited from his mother.

It's been a month Drona is still in the coma. Rick comes to visit him now and then. The vast and mighty soul of Ravana needed time to mend in the little body. The poison was no more affecting him, his body was capable of absorbing venom.

Every night Abdus pulled the couch near Drona's bed and read him the stories his son loved. One night, while he was pulling the furniture, he heard a moaning sound. He turned back and saw him sleeping like a baby. He sat on the couch, opened the marked the page of Miss. Rumphius by Barbara Cooney and started reading to him "Sun come up she watched it cross the heavens and sparkle on the water, and she saw it set in glory in the evening she started a little garden among the rocks that surrounded her house, and she planted a few flower seeds in the stony—"

After reading a while, he looked at Drona and saw him sitting on the bed. He was finally awake. The sudden action of the little boy made Abdus scared for a moment. Then he hugged him tightly, though he wasn't sure whether he was hugging his son or Ravana.

"How are you feeling, son?" he asked.

"I am feeling good papa," he replied in the same sound like his son but with a different tone, confident and matured.

"Are you hungry?"

Drona pushed back his curly hair from his forehead and nodded.

Abdus ignored his instinct, "Come On! I will make you something to eat; you must be hungry." tickling him in his stomach.

Drona laughed and nodded gain. He picked him up in his arms and went to the kitchen and made him sit on the kitchen slab and started cutting off the crust from the bread. Drona never liked the crust on his sandwich.

Drona jumped down on the floor and went to the refrigerator, twice he opened and closed the door, felt cheered about the icy gas coming out of it and the light turning on whenever he opened the door and going off as he closed it. He took out a piece of eyes from the freezer and put it in his mouth, rolling it all over inside. He started walking down the drawing room, touching and feeling the furniture, the lamp, the heat of the light bulb, frequently switching the tube light off and on, continually staring at the motion of the fan. He watched his feet stepping on the rug. Raised his nose, sniffing the fresh air then he stopped at the frame of him and his parents hanging on the wall. He touched the picture of Abeedah turned towards Abdus and said

"Papa I know mom is gone and she will never come back. But I miss her. I miss her calling my name." he said with tears dripping from his eyes.

Confused Abdus bend down to him, with a gentle hug he said, "I miss her too, son." he took a deep sobbing breathe, opened his eyes and asked curiously "But how do you know that?"

"I saw everything. I was there," he replied.

Before he could ask Drona another question, the door bell rang. Abdus handed him the sandwich and walked to the door. He watched from the peephole; it was Rick. He opened the door warmly and welcomed him inside. Since he brought his son back to life, they had developed a friendly relationship. He trusted him with Drona.

Rick walked inside and saw Drona sitting on the couch eating his sandwich. Drona looked at Rick and said, "I am glad to see you here, son. Want to have a bite?"

For Abdus it was freaky, to hear his son calling Rick, son. Rick stood in front of him like a loyal soldier. "I am glad to see you too, father."

"I am proud of you son; you did the righteous thing. You honored me by morally obligated to intervene your brother's intentions." Drona said to Rick.

"Is there any command for me, father?"

"Yes, I want to have a long talk with you but after I spend some solitude time with myself and my father," he said pointing at Abdus.

"As you say, father," Rick said and left them alone.

Abdus stunned with their talk, sat beside Drona quietly for awhile and then asked "What do you remember? Are you my son or their father?"

"I am both. I remember everything. The weight of the sword in my hand and the weight of my books. The power I possessed and the partial vision without my glasses, abducting someone's wife and getting punished by mother after every mistake I made. I remember the taste of wine and also remember the taste of mother's milk in my mouth. I remember being vicious also remember being naive, I remember being a great scholar also remember making spelling mistakes in my homework, I remember being the noble king of Lanka and also remember being your son." He replied wisely without any hesitation, looking into Abdus's eyes.

Abdus didn't know how to react. He didn't know how to deal with the situation. He suggested Drona take rest and get some sleep and he took him to his bed, tugged him properly and without saying anything, he left the room. He wanted to calm down but couldn't stop freaking out. He was still not sure about Drona. He was his son, even talks like him, but he was changed inside.

Chapter Twenty eight

The court of guardians

The night was still long and cold with lots of unexpected secrets locked inside its chest. Abdus took out pints of beer from the refrigerator and started drinking. Even after three empty bottles, he felt troubled. The beer was not helping him anymore. Since Abeedah's death, her memory haunted him in the bedroom, he started sleeping on the couch.

As he rested his head on the sofa, the door bell rang again. He rubbed his eyes and opened the door, saw Apollo standing on the door step and gave him a loud answer by slammed the door on his face. Apollo being Apollo, zapped himself inside and said: "What was that behavior, don't you have respect for your adults or GODS?"

"I don't want to see you, get out of my house." Abdus said furiously.

"Your house? Since when cavemen own a house?"

The word 'Caveman' struck his guts because Abeedah was the only one who used to call him Caveman.

"Yes, I know she used to call you that. I am not here to rub salt in your open wound but pay my condolences."

"I don't want any condolence from you. You did it; you provoked Abeedah to do such insane thing. She would have been alive if it wasn't for you. Also, my son is sleeping; he shouldn't be disturbed."

Apollo knew an angry mind is stubborn enough to block all the doors of hearing. Apollo touched his hand, and the next moment, Abdus found himself walking on the lonely street. The roads were ghost-quite without a single vehicle running, the lampposts were the only means of light to the street. Without the traffic, he could hear the crickets making noise. A white line ran down the center, relatively unbroken compared to the scarred and potholed concrete.

The wind was howling like some horror movie opener. All that remains is the concrete structures themselves, no glass, no wood, nothings the scavengers could use. With all the stress, with all the many times he wished to be alone, it was home, Funny. He always thought the home was a place, now home is a feeling, and that feeling at their apartment died with Abeedah. Although, Anger was all he could feel at that moment, it was soothing to get away from all the chaos for a moment. But Apollo was a God for a reason. His aura was similar to getting a glimpse of sun on a shivering winter day.

"I know you like it here. Away from everything, even for a moment. Holding onto anger will be like you drinking the poison and expecting me to die from it. And no offence but we both know that is impossible." Apollo said to lighten Ashwatthama's mood.

After walking few steps further with Ashwatthama's cold expression he said, "I helped her. If she hadn't had sacrificed herself now, she would have to born again and again, relive the same painful life, again and again, to seek for the moment just like this. She was a cursed soul just like you, Ashwatthama.

Remember what Vidura once quoted to Kavya, to save a family, abandon a man; to save the village, abandon a family; to save the country, abandon a village; to protect the soul, abandon the earth. She abandons earth to save his son's soul." Apollo explained calmly.

Furthermore he narrated him Abeedah's story and why she needed to sacrifices herself. After hearing to which, all his anger vanished, knowing that her beloved wife is resting in peace. Though he would give anything to go back, back to their life as it was once, a normal but happy family of three.

"If you know everything, then you must defiantly know what happened to Manik and where is he now?" Abdus asked skeptically.

"Yes, I know what happened to him, and I also know where he is now. But I would suggest leaving it to his family. Let his family worry about him." Apollo replied skeptically.

"Why?"

Apollo raised his eyebrow; he was not sure about the quote.

"I mean why did you intervene, why are you so interested in our life?" Abdus asked suspiciously.

Apollo chuckled softly and replied, "Sun must guide the direction to the travelers, and that's what I am doing.

Things happen for a reason, if you haven't had committed the crime of killing an unborn, you wouldn't have been cursed, if you weren't cursed, you wouldn't have met your wife, and if you wouldn't have met your wife, Ravana had no chance to walk the earth. There is a bigger war coming, a war this world has never seen.

Every war needs sacrifice, but this one will be a massacre. You both will play an essential role in that war. I don't know which side you will fight, but it is defiantly going to happen."

"I just wanna know if he is Ravana or my son?" Abdus asked Apollo.

"That is a puzzle that you and only you can solve, nobody else," Apollo said and vanished into thin air. Abdus found himself on his drawing stand where he was, near the door. He went to the couch, held the half-empty can of beer and took a sip. Between all the conversations the beer lost its chill. He threw the cans one by one the dustbin, like shoot the basketball on the hoop and led his head on the couch while thinking about what Apollo said.

The doorbell rang for the third time. The night had no intentions of passing by quietly. With every door bell, his troubled mind was getting new surprises which sunk him into the pool of dilemmas and confusion. Every step he took towards the door he wanted to go back to his couch and sleep, shutting off his eyes by plugging in some music loud enough not to hear the door bell, again. But being an ancient person and coming from a family of Brahmins, who touch him since childhood "Atithi Devo Bhava." He didn't want to disrespect any guest by sending them back from the door.

He opened the door, and got the last and most prominent element of surprise, which was likely to be unbelievable. He had the shock registered on his face before he could hide it. His brain cogs couldn't turn fast enough to take in the information from her wide eyes.

He saw KripaCharya, his long-lost uncle from the days of Mahabharata, whom he saw after an era, he is the epitomes of the virtue of impartiality. Though he was aware that the Kauravas were resorting to immoral ways, he impartially carried out his duty and proved his gratitude to the Kauravas as they nurtured him with food and shelter in the palace.

He was considered very special since in the first place he was not born from the human womb like any other human being and directly emanated from the semen of his father Shardwan that fell on to the ground. He had secured a vital place in the epic of Mahabharata by his strict adherence to values.

Immortality was conferred on him by Lord Krishna through a blessing. He was prioritized for the conference of immortality even above Dronacharya since he demonstrated some great virtues like truth, righteousness, and impartiality. Even under highly stressful conditions he was not prepared to compromise with his values, and in this regard, he stood out as the noblest among men.

"Uncle Kripa?" he said stock. He couldn't believe his eyes.

He pushed his oval bipolar glass up to the bridge of his nose and said "Hello!"

Distressed Abdus said, "After showing yourself after an era, this is what you say 'Hello,'? Where were you when I needed you? Do you even know what I went through?"

"You have all the reasons to be disappointed and angry with me. But I never abandoned you. I have always been watching over you and your family, son. Not only because I promised your mother, my sister but I always considered you as my own. I always loved you as my own.

I stayed away because I was bound with my duties. But I tried to warn your wife of what was coming, but you chose to ignore and see what happened. Your mother connected us with an empathy link, so that, I always know when you are in trouble." He replied.

Abdus recalled Abeedah mentioning an old man working her about the baby and al the incidence whose were relevant to what he said.

He asked, "You saved me from those Cambions?"

Kripa's facial expression confirmed his doubt, "Yes and I also saved you from the chaos you created in the country. I was the one who sent you those IDs."

"Then why did you disappear? Why didn't you show yourself to me?" Abdus asked.

"We are not alone. We are being watched over by someone. Someone who knows who we are and he know where we are. The chief of Court of Guardians has send me to find you." Kripa explained.

"Court of Guardians?"

"Yes, Ved Vyasa. He is gathering everyone for the war."

Suddenly, they heard Drona's voice calling from behind standing near the hallway "Papa!"

Abdus turned around, and behind him, he saw Kripacharya and shouted with excitement "Acharya sir!" and jumped over him.

"Hello Drona, it's good to see you," he said by hugging him close.

"You are his Acharya sir? Can't say I am surprised to hear this now." Abdus said.

"Told you I have been watching over you and your family," Kripa said laying his hand on Drona's head.

"You two know each other" Drona asked pointing the finger at both of them.

Abdus on his one knee held his tiny hand and said, "He is your grandfather, Drona."

"I came here for you Drona," he said looking at Drona and shifted his eyes towards Ashwatthama "When Abeedah brought back Ravana's soul to Drona's body, someone escaped out of that portal when the veil was put down, somebody evil who was caged for a very long time by the Gods. Now he has started building his army, and we have to be prepared."

"Who?" Abdus asked.

Kripa saw a crow sitting outside the window behind the glass, staring at them. Agitated Kripa said, "I will have to leave now" and starts walking towards the door.

"But uncle Krip—"

"I will visit you soon. Till then don't ignore the gravity of the situation." he slammed the door behind him.

Abdus had so many questions in mind. He couldn't process the Drona's situation, and now Kripacharya also left him with an abrupt answer, leaving behind a big question mark. His brain was flooding with all the unsolved puzzles. It was a delicious moment where his face washed blank with confusion. He could only sleep when exhausted. He felt the tiredness in her chest, in how she breathed and her thoughts dragged by in slow motion, he slunk to a quiet spot and curled himself on the couch. Time has taken on a different form, more plentiful than ever it was, and more quiet moments to think through the oblivion of sleep would be kinder. He was craving for rest, but the questions haunted him as a ghost as he tried to close his eyes. Finally unable to sleep he opened his eyes and sat on the couch. He stretched his neck left and right to release at least a pinch of stress from his shoulder and saw Drona quietly standing near the wall, glancing at him, eyes filled with innocence and duck printed off white night suit.

"Papa, I am not able to sleep either."

"What you want me to do?" his voice sounded stressed.

"I want to listen to the song, the one you always play for me. It always put drag me to sleep" He said.

Drona took out the record from his shelf and played "Broomstick cowboy." He sat in the rocking chair. Drona ran and sat on his lap, resting his head on Abdus's chest. Just like old days. At that very instance, the clouds of doubled fogged away. Abdus knew, he might be having the soul of Ravana keeping him alive, he might have his memory, but undoubtedly he was still his beloved son Drona. Drona, whose eyes will always remind him of his mother, the love of his life, Abeedah. He patted his hand softy and started singing the song along with the record.

Dream on, little broomstick cowboy,
Of rocket ships and Mars
On sunny days,
And Willie Mays,
And chocolate candy bars

Dream on, little broomstick cowboy,
Dream while you can
Of big green frogs,
And puppy dogs,
And castles in the sand

For, all too soon you'll awaken

Your toys will all be gone
Your broomstick horse will ride away,
To find another home
And you'll have grown into a man,
With cowboys of your own
And then you'll have to go to war,
To try and save your home
And then you'll have to learn to hate
You'll have to learn to kill
It's always been that way, my son
I guess it always will
No broomstick gun they'll hand you
No longer you'll pretend
You'll call some man your enemy
You used to call him 'friend.'
And when the rockets thunder,
You'll hear your brothers cry
And through it all, you'll wonder
Just why they had to die

So dream on, little broomstick cowboy,
Dream while you can
For soon, you'll be a dreadful thing
My son, you'll be a man

The indescribable love between a father and a son, was the beginning of Ashwatthama's story and reason for his curse and the same love brought him back from the same curse. The love that never make any quote, the love which never comes to any attention, which is always comes second in a queue, is the love which makes a child strong. A father does not express his love to become a teacher and to guide his life with the tough rules which makes him a man.

A mother's heart is a deep abyss at the bottom of which a child always find forgiveness but a father's heart always desires his child to stand tall against the world and walk fearlessly. Ashwatthama was now both father and mother of Drona.

Drona wrapped his hand around Abdus's pinky and slept. A father never says how much he loves his son, but when the time comes, he can fight the world to protect him. He said looking at his sleeping eyes, "Doesn't matter who you are but the truth I am your father and I will give you the love and guidance which I received from my father. My curse was broken, the day I held you in my hand but today I am free from being the servant of the eternal."